Peace with Trees

a memoir

Susannah Pitman

Soleil Press

RANDOLPH, NEW JERSEY

Susannah Pitman/Soleil Press

susannahpitman@gmail.com

www.susannahpitman.com

Book Layout © 2017 BookDesignTemplates.com

Cover design by Gus Yoo

Copy editing by Stephanie Gunning

Peace with Trees/Susannah Pitman. —1st ed.

ISBN 978-0-9997128-0-1

Library of Congress Control Number 2017919378

To Mom and Dad

Contents

Author's Note

Out of respect for their privacy, I have changed the
names of some of the people who appear in these pages.

CHAPTER 1

A Thousand Cardboard Boxes

EVERYTHING WENT SIDEWAYS in a second. It had been a perfectly beautiful August day—sunshine, warmth, stillness. Nothing moved. Nothing wanted to. It was a day that wanted to take a nap after reading a good book while lounging in the shade next to a table with a slippery, wet glass of sweet iced tea. A day where time moved comfortably slow, allowing every moment to be savored, the sun perfectly content to stay in one place and shine light over our yellow 1830's farmhouse.

We didn't live on a farm. What once had been a farm was now a development of split-level and bilevel homes. Our house was memorable, sitting on the street corner, its yard lined with a stone wall dotted with purple puddingstone and featuring a well with a working pulley and wooden bucket and an old maple tree right by the driveway, my favorite of the many trees that stood tall throughout our yard.

The maple tree had a massive limb that swung out gracefully from the trunk. As a child, I wanted to climb the tree and sit on that limb, but it was a little too high for my comfort. Instead, I opted to sit on a large root that emerged from the base, the perfect size for a little one's chair. It was there that I sat and collected leaves in the fall, rested from building snow forts in the winter, traced the roots and bark with my fingers in the spring, and watched cars drive by in the summer, the limb freely stretching outward right above me. Near the base of the limb was an opening, a scar from a past injury, where squirrels, chipmunks, and occasionally raccoons scurried in and out, perhaps living communally and finding their own pockets of space within the vast hollow trunk. It seemed large enough to accommodate all of them without conflict.

In essence, for the first twenty years of my life, I

lived with my family in a storybook setting in the storybook town of Denville in northern New Jersey, where life was simple until everything went sideways.

My dad and I sat in the TV room watching the New York Yankees play the Texas Rangers, he in his blue recliner with Mickey, our obese tuxedo tiger cat, curled up on his lap, me on the matching plaid couch with my feet propped up on the white wicker chest that served as a coffee table. We wished we were at the stadium given how beautiful it was outside. It would have been a great way to spend my last day at home before I returned to Syracuse University for my junior year. Instead, we had completed errands— mundane things like going to the car wash and the pharmacy, nothing that matched what the day wanted us to do.

The TV beeped, and a scrolling message appeared at the bottom of the screen. Severe weather was coming. My dad and I looked at each other, surprised since the few fluffy clouds that floated in the sky appeared stationary, not a breeze anywhere to push anything. His newly cleaned cream Cadillac Seville was parked in the driveway. He pulled the handle on his recliner to release the foot rest, an automatic signal to Mickey that he was to wake up and jump down. He stood up and walked out the door, I assumed to move his car into the garage.

Mickey crept over to me and jumped up on my lap, head butting my face with affection before doing his usual turn around to curl up and settle in. It was the bottom of the first inning. Bernie Williams had just hit a double deep into center field, when the phone rang. I let it ring a few times, not wanting to disturb Mickey and hoping my mom would get it. By the third ring, it was clear that she was occupied doing something, perhaps folding laundry or dusting or any number of tasks she did regularly to add to our wonderful home life. I patted Mickey, my signal to him that I had to get up. He reluctantly hopped down and sat in the middle of the floor, as if waiting for one of us to return so he could regain a spot on someone's lap. I got up and raced to the phone before the answering machine kicked on. It was one of my dad's golf buddies.

I walked out onto the porch with the cordless phone. The sun was shining, splotches of bright blue sky peeking through white fluffy clouds, the same clouds that hadn't seemed to move all day. My dad had already put his car into the garage and was in the middle of the driveway, having walked out to the mailbox to get the mail, when the stillness and the mundane quality of the day was disrupted.

Without any warning that it was coming other than that scrolling message at the bottom of the TV a few minutes beforehand, a strong gust of wind suddenly blew in from the west. It built on itself, gaining momentum exponentially, roaring in like a jet engine. The sky darkened. The clear air turned to a murky brownish gray. What had been standing tall was now bending over at a right angle. Leaves whipped like flags, their stems holding on with all their might, the weaker ones choosing to let go and float away. Treetops freakishly curved eastward. The grass flattened. My mom's brown Buick, parked in front of the porch, quivered.

The tree with the massive limb was the first victim, its scar forecasting that it never had a chance. With this wind, the limb ripped away from the trunk, making a sound that will forever stay with me: *a thousand cardboard boxes ripping at once*. The sound penetrated me, stiffening my body, instinctually freezing it in place on the porch. The limb's heaviness landed on the second victim, my mom's car, causing the trunk to crumple up like aluminum foil, the glass to shatter, and the front to violently bounce up and down. My dad, in the direct path of this flying limb, had only a moment to look up and shield his head with his arm as the sticks and leaves crashed into him. Then I could no longer see him.

It all happened in less than a second.

A drenching rain followed. Through the phone, I screamed at my dad's golf buddy to hang up so I could call 9-1-1. He thought I was joking and wouldn't disconnect. Desperately, I roared at him to hang up while I repeatedly pressed the end button. Still no dial tone. Again, I shouted at my dad's golf buddy, wanting my voice to choke him so that he would understand that nothing about this was a joke. I finally heard a dial tone and called 9-1-1.

I screamed for my mom through the screen door, who casually came around the corner of the hallway into the dining room, unaware that anything had happened and rushing only when she finally saw me. I opened the screen door and pulled her onto the porch, pointing toward my dad, who was invisible underneath the limb. She gasped at the scene—the tree, her car—but didn't see why I kept pointing.

"WHAT?" she pleaded. "What's wrong? What? What?"

I had lost the ability to speak. All I could do was point. I led my mom toward the edge of the porch, unable to step off and bring her to him. I didn't want to see any more than I'd already seen.

Dad was completely obstructed. My mom couldn't understand. She kept asking me what was wrong. It took everything in me to push the words out of my mouth, like in a dream where you want to scream and you have no voice, so I couldn't speak. I kept pointing and crying, and was now trembling uncontrollably.

Mom made her way closer and ran toward the sticks and leaves, at which point she finally saw his prone body. She crouched down next to him among the branches. She screamed at me to come and help, but I couldn't move.

"THIS IS YOUR FATHER! YOU'VE GOT TO HELP HIM!" she shouted to me.

My legs felt like jelly. I held the side of the house as I stepped off the porch into the pounding rain and unforgiving wind. I couldn't walk. I may have crawled

SUSANNAH PITMAN

to her. I didn't want to see. *Is Dad alive or dead?* I didn't know.

My mom tapped my dad, trying to rouse him. Kneeling next to my mom, I could now see. Pinned under branches, sticks, and leaves, he was flat on his back, his head turned slightly to the side, glasses knocked off, eyes open and staring vacantly ahead, mail strewn all about him. I still didn't know.

My mom shouted at me to get towels. I ran inside, my legs becoming a powerful escape vehicle. I would have done anything to get away from seeing him, but I also knew that getting towels would be my way to help him. Running into the house, my safe haven for twenty years, helped me get away from what had just happened. It was an attempt to rewind the clock, wake up from the nightmare, or desperately do anything possible to change what couldn't be changed. In the linen closet, I found a large stack of neatly folded white bath towels. I grabbed the entire stack and ran back toward the front door, my legs again losing their power the closer I got.

"I CALLED 9-1-1," I yelled to my mom as thunder crashed around us.

"WHERE ARE THEY? KEEP CALLING UNTIL THEY GET HERE!"

I ran back to the porch and grabbed the cordless phone that I had set down on the red bench and called 9-1-1 again, another thing to do to help while still avoiding seeing. The dispatcher said help was already on the way. Seconds felt like minutes. I still couldn't move back to my mom to help, still afraid to see, to know the answer to alive or dead. I called Kurt and Marilyn, my dad's law practice partner and his wife, who lived down the street from us. They got there just before five police officers pulled up.

Five sets of flashing lights. These were joined by more lights: two ambulances, two fire trucks, and a sea of cars with blue flashing lights. Dissonant red, white, and blue flashes, lighting up the wet, gray air, magnified the horror of what didn't need to be any bigger. Several dozen first responders carried first aid supplies, others finding saws and axes to cut away the downed tree limb. From within the chaos word traveled to me that my dad was conscious.

Many people worked together to free my dad as the rain pounded and lightning stuck too close for comfort. Some familiar faces emerged through the flashes of emergency lights. Kim, a volunteer rushing toward my dad while carrying medical supplies, made eye contact with me and released a deep breath, breaking her focus for one moment to convey to me that she knew this was bad. Up to this point, she was only known to me as the girl I had ridden on the bus with to Girl Scout camp. In middle school, we took tap lessons together. I remember that I accidentally scratched her brand-new black, high-heeled tap shoes while horsing around before class. Although she had been annoyed, she didn't cry about it. She shook off her upset seconds later as we laughed about other things.

Willie, a classmate throughout my schooling, was one of the guys lifting the stretcher that was carrying my dad. He had been held back a year as a young kid, so we met in second grade, the grade he was repeating. A few times I saw him teased by other boys for no apparent reason and watched him cry. Yet somehow the bullying never affected his heart enough to stop him from caring about others. He was kind. Even though I never hung out with Willie in high school, having parked right behind me in the school parking lot one January morning, he decided to follow me home, without me asking, the first time I ever drove in a snowstorm, just to make sure I was safe. Now, he avoided eye contact, even though he knew who the man on the stretcher was. Many of the EMTs and volunteers swarming our yard had used my dad for real estate closings, small business formations, and the writing of their wills. If they didn't know him as an attorney, they knew him as a former member of the Board of Education. If not from there, then as a volunteer at the annual Harvest Festival. If not that, then as the parent of one of their kid's classmates.

Now they'd know him as the guy who was hit by a tree.

THE WAITING AREA in the emergency room was crowded, or so it felt. There were some empty chairs, but not enough for me to sit far enough away from strangers to get privacy. After crying for hours, tears were stinging my face. I could not stop them from flowing. As the only one in the room constantly crying, others stole quick glances my way, wondering what had happened.

We knew my dad was alive, but we didn't know anything else for hours. Then we found out that his lower vertebrae were shattered. Surgery was scheduled for the next morning, a Sunday. Special equipment needed to be flown in from Ohio overnight. Meanwhile, the surgeon and his team were preparing themselves for what could be a ten-hour surgery, all in an attempt to prevent or minimize paralysis.

I imagined how Dad's life in a wheelchair would be. No more golf. Getting on a boat to go fishing would be challenging. My parents would need to move to another house, one better suited for an extra-large wheelchair to fit his six-foot-two, 300-plus-pound body. I would take the semester off to aid him in his recovery. Different scenarios played out in my mind. We would have tough times, but we would manage. We'd grow closer. My dad would eat healthier. He'd lose weight. It would be okay.

After the doctors stabilized my dad and finished evaluating him, we were able to see him. I was so upset that I could barely walk. The last I had seen of him, he was on the stretcher being pushed into the ambulance. He had winced at every jostle, the pain was so intense. I held on to my mom, who somehow had strength to hold me up, as we now walked toward the doorway of his hospital room and up to his hospital bed, still afraid to see. I used the side rails on the bed to support myself, to show my dad strength from the waist up while my legs shook with fear and sadness below his line of sight.

He looked dirty and flecks of leaves were still stuck to his hands and face. Underneath him I caught a glimpse of familiar fabric. It was the shirt he had been wearing, which was now in tatters from being cut away to facilitate emergency treatment. Dried blood caked his elbow. A few of his teeth were knocked out, making it difficult to understand him; his voice not sounding like his usual authoritative, slightly lawyerish dad voice. Weakness, pain, vulnerability. Nothing about this was like him.

"I'm hurt real bad," he said. He didn't think he was going to make it. He cried as he told us this. He couldn't believe his pain. One moment he was getting the mail and the next he was pinned under a tree in the middle of a storm. His short-term memory didn't register what happened, so we told him. He still couldn't believe it, even though I could. It was the constant background music in my head—*a thousand cardboard boxes ripping at once.*

We told him he would make it. Inside, I pleaded with him not to give up. He had to make it. I was only twenty. He needed to see me graduate college. He needed to walk me down the aisle when I got married. He needed to take his grandkids fishing. He was only fifty-three.

Unable to stay next to my dad, I went back to the waiting area. I didn't want him to see me so broken, to worry about me when he needed to focus on getting better. My body shook, recalling what happened. The wind. The tree. *A thousand cardboard boxes ripping at once.* That sound was in me, as if it had vibrated deep inside and formed a marker on my DNA. It consumed my thoughts along with my dad. I could think of nothing else.

Without realizing what I was doing, I found myself rocking in my seat like a drug addict going through withdrawal. I noticed this after I saw several concerned eyes staring at me in the emergency room. I stopped, shocked at what I was doing. *I'm not crazy.*

I saw something horrible. That's all. The eyes darted away every time I met their gaze.

A crushing sensation built inside my core as if the tree had punched me in the gut. I wanted to vomit, but I hadn't eaten in over nine hours. Instead, my body returned to rocking, my arms crossed tightly across my stomach, my shoulders rounding forward as if I was protecting my heart, keeping it from exploding from trauma.

The doctors continued to tend to my dad while my mom and I sat in the waiting room. Rarely were the two of us ever silent when we were together. So often we were thinking the same things and finishing each other's sentences. She was never one to cry in front of me or ever reveal any vulnerability. She was always the one I'd run to for comfort, and she'd always have the right words to say to me. My mom, always perfectly composed with the right outfit and makeup, even while spending the day at home cleaning and cooking, now showed small cracks in her demeanor. She held back her tears, but I could tell with her watery eyes and deep breaths it was a struggle for her to do so, just as it was a struggle for me not to rock. As easy and effortless as our relationship had always been, now we didn't know what to say to each other. I suggested we each call someone for support.

My mom called Aunt Janice, my dad's youngest sister. She immediately drove up from South Plainfield. She was a nurse and also the closest relative, geographically. She helped interpret what the doctors told us, which I couldn't register at all.

I called Kristine, a high school friend who was studying nursing. She hadn't gone back to school yet for the fall, so without hesitation she met me in the ER along with Dan and Ann Marie, two other friends who were with her when I called. I explained what had happened over the phone. She couldn't believe it.

The doctors needed my dad's hypertension medications, so Kristine drove me, Dan and Ann Marie home to pick them up. Returning home, we found the driveway miraculously cleared of everything except my mom's crumpled brown Buick and the heavy base of the offending tree limb that remained resting on the car's trunk. Later, I learned that four neighbors had gathered together to clean everything up. Two plastic bags of latex gloves, gauze, tubes, and other medical waste I couldn't identify sat on the porch ready to be properly disposed of. I left them, unsure of what to do with them. Some of the waste was splattered with dried blood. On the bench lay my dad's glasses, the lenses now cracked.

The broken maple tree stood fragile, lit only by the street light. It looked like a ghost, the bark forming wavy shadows, its hollow center more cavernous than I had ever imagined. This once beautiful tree had shown its vulnerability with that perfectly round scar that to me had always appeared as a beauty mark, a weakness we had all ignored. With only half of the tree still standing, it looked like it hovered over our house. I was afraid to go near the tree.

I unlocked the door and turned on the dining room light. Walking into the house was like crossing through the barrier between what is and what was. It looked like nothing had happened. Everything was still in its place. Blue tapered candles stood tall in the pewter chambersticks. Wooden toy blocks from my mother's childhood spelled out "summer fun" on the shelf above the drawers of the antique dry sink. Fine china, my mom and dad's wedding gift, which had been used for holidays for nearly thirty years, displayed its unique gray and rust pattern among the crystal stemware and tea leaf serving pieces.

Turning right into the kitchen, I turned on the lights, continuing to move through what was—oak cabinets, cream textured Formica countertops, linoleum flooring patterned to look like tan bricks, the butcher block kitchen table where we ate dinner as a family together every night. His medications were in the antique wooden hutch, the one my parents had bought and refinished early in their marriage. I grabbed the bottles.

Turning around, I noticed Mickey's food and water bowls in their usual place on the floor next to the peninsula. The wet food had dried and was untouched. At twenty-three pounds, Mickey loved food. It was way past his usual dinner time. I hadn't seen him since I got up from the couch. I picked up his food dish and tossed the old food, replacing it with fresh canned food, his favorite tuna-based flavor. Normally, he would raise his head at the sound of the cabinet door opening and would only come running when he heard his food can being lifted from the shelf. He could recognize that this can sounded different from the sounds of the soup cans, the spices, the peanut butter jars, and all the other pantry items that were stacked on the Lazy Susan. Despite that subtle, familiar sound, he didn't appear. *Where is he?* I wondered.

While my friends stayed in the kitchen, I went looking for him in his usual lounging spots. He wasn't on the recliner in the TV room. He wasn't on the blue Ethan Allen armchair in the living room. He wasn't on his favorite blue blanket on my mom and dad's bed. I looked up the stairs, and became over-whelmed by a sense of fear, believing the tree could fall and strike that part of the house at any moment—possibly crashing through the roof. I knew he might have been up there on one of the beds, maybe on my bed. My bedroom, the place that would immediately come to mind and where I wanted to go whenever I was scared during my childhood, now became a place I was afraid to go.

At the bottom of the stairs, I thought of his other hiding place: the crawl space next to the basement steps that led down to his litter box. I turned on the stairway light and stepped down. Peering under the wooden utility shelves I saw two wide, shiny cat eyes staring up at me. He was just around the corner from his food dish. He must have heard those sounds that signified food, yet stayed put. I reached in and pulled him out, reassuring him that everything would be okay. Somehow, he knew.

NOTHING CHANGED WHEN we returned to the hospital. In between doctors, my mom and I made our way to my dad's bedside, my mom staying with him more than me. Aunt Janice was also with my dad constantly. I could barely stand up. Most of the time I sat in the waiting room, quietly rocking, trying to stop myself from crying. I rocked in front of everyone who was with us. It felt crazy to do so but good at the same time. I didn't care what anyone thought.

My mom came back to the waiting area while the doctors needed to tend to my dad. As we sat together, a face with a jaw dropped and eyes wide open came around the corner and looked directly at me. I tapped my mom's thigh and motioned for her to look up at who was coming. I'm not sure if it was from her or me, but I heard a groan of *oh god*. I stopped rocking, my posture snapping up in alignment. A woman

slowly started to make her way down the short hallway to us. I didn't recognize her immediately, but it
was clear that she was looking for us. Her expression
revealed that she knew what had happened. After a
few seconds of quickly scrolling through my mind
trying to think of who this woman might be, it hit me.
She was the mom of my sister's childhood friend. She
was with a man I assumed was her husband, someone I had seen maybe twice in my whole life. My mom
and dad were not particularly close with this couple.
They weren't at our backyard picnics eating hamburgers and playing whiffle ball. I never saw my mom
and dad go to dinner with them. I never knew my
mom and this woman to go out for a day of shopping.
Still, here they were, seeking us out at the hospital, a
completely unexpected show of support that felt in-
vasive. It turned out that they had heard what happened through their emergency scanner.

I didn't want them there. I didn't want our family's
private moments to be theirs as well. I didn't want
them to see my dad and I didn't want them to see me
like this: crying, rocking, and falling apart. I imagined how baffled my dad would be after telling him

they came to visit. They felt like spectators to our family's tragedy.

The intrusive couple stayed longer than expected. I could barely process their presence let alone what they were saying. The man stood in front of where I sat, my eyes frequently catching a glimpse of his fly halfway down. I wanted to tell him his zipper was open, but couldn't form the words as it took all of my energy to keep from rocking and crying. I put on a calm facade, not wanting to share an ounce of my pain with them. When they asked what had happened, I shared as few details as possible. I didn't want to give them anything.

I don't know how long they stayed, but as they finally walked away and rounded the corner, Dan broke the ice. "Did anyone else notice that his fly was down?"

Everyone laughed, nodding in agreement, including me. It broke through the barriers I had put up to contain myself. Stillness followed for a while and then my body quietly returned to rocking without me realizing it.

MY DAD WAS ADMITTED into intensive care. Rocking continued, back and forth . . . back and forth . . . smoothing out the turmoil that stirred inside me. He was stable, but not out of the woods. Surgery was all set for 8:00 am the next morning.

It felt okay to leave him at the hospital after Aunt Janice agreed to stay with him the entire night—as okay as could be. As a nurse, she made the situation feel more stable. A long road lay ahead, and something had to stop the pattern that was forming, stop the rocking, stop this cycle. Aunt Janice could handle things that night, giving my mom a break and me a chance to calm down.

Kristine drove us home and stayed with us, offering to take us back to the hospital in the morning. Creeping into the house at close to midnight, we only had a few hours before the surgery to get some sleep. Looking out a window at the remainder of the tree standing unbalanced and threatening near the house, I feared going to bed. My own room didn't feel

safe. Fear of the rest of the tree or of other trees falling consumed me. Disturbing sounds repeated in my
head: the roar of the wind, the crumpling of the car,
the sirens of the ambulances. The loudest one, *a thousand cardboard boxes ripping at once,* made me shake.
Flashing lights speckled a visual memory of the limb
hitting my dad. I couldn't stop thinking about it.

My mom allowed me to spend the night next to her
lying where my dad was supposed to be sleeping. She
didn't seem to mind that I talked to myself all night
as I stared wide-eyed at the ceiling. I made up stories
to calm myself, a stream of consciousness to take me
away from where I was.

*I want to go somewhere. Where? Away from here. Any-
where but here. I don't want to be here. I don't want this.
This. This really happened. This can't be happening. I don't
want to be here. Go somewhere. Anywhere. Go. My favorite
place . . . imagine myself there.*

Beach. Sand. Waves. Shells.

Go there.

*I am lying on the warm beach, my muscles melting on
the hot sand. Tension eases, I sink inward . . . into its soft
mounds, which are holding me.*

My neck relaxes.

My back relaxes.
My breath relaxes.
My mind relaxes.
Relax . . . breathe.
Looking out at the playful sea . . .
Waves crashing again and again . . .
Again and again. Again and again.
The sweet rhythm will calm me down.
I paddle out to catch a wave, to sail away, fly, and escape.
I wait for it . . . I wait for it.
A perfect send off from the now, it catches me and takes me away on a thrilling ride, gliding, splashing.
Nature is propelling me to shore.
Free as a fish, free as a bird . . .
A bird in the sky, flying high . . .
The night sky to the moon and stars, which get closer as the earth gets smaller.
Floating. Vanishing. Up I go.
Up I go. Up I go.
Silence.
Space.
Calm.
Peace.
Heaven? No . . . not heaven. But what?

Freedom.

Now . . . in space . . . now . . . it's not so bad.

Beauty. Sparkly. Twinkling. Dark.

The darkness magnifying the light . . . the spark . . . of life that's still here.

I whispered to myself until the night sky grew lighter, time marching toward the surgery. Just as I had calmed myself down the anticipation of the day ahead leaked into my mind. My nerves trembled as I was confronted with a thought I had never previously entertained: *What if this is the last time I ever see him?*

BRAVE FACE. ALL MORNING. Not a wink of sleep. Not an ounce of hunger. I showered, wanting to wash everything away. I put on jeans, a tee-shirt, and flip flops.

No crying. No rocking. Calm. *Up I go.*

I told myself the day would be okay. I shoved the *what if* away. Telling became convincing, which turned into arguing, which turned into a battle within my chest as the fear of the *what if* kept rising to the surface. I did everything I could to push it down, to squash it, to stop it from coloring the day, the surgery, the future. But the battle was lost while walking down the hallway toward my dad's room. With less than thirty feet to go, I collapsed on the floor in a heap of uncontrollable hysterics.

My mom and Kristine knelt down next to me, urging me to get up. We only had minutes before my dad would be wheeled out to the operating room. I didn't want to face the moment—the one I feared could be our last living moment together. I wanted to stop time, to physically pull it back to sitting in the TV room watching the Yankee game. I have never wanted something more in my entire life.

Kristine ran down the hallway toward my dad's room to make sure we still had time. "Susie, you have to get up," my mom pleaded. "Daddy would really like to see you before the surgery."

A battle raged inside me. I wanted desperately to stop the question from arising, but it was inevitable. *What if this is the last time?* I had to face my fear. I forced some deep breaths and stood up, leaning on my mom for the remaining thirty feet it took to get to my dad's room. Every step toward the door felt closer to that possible once-in-a-lifetime moment, a moment I had never imagined until that morning. I sucked in all the shaking and the tears, hoping that it wouldn't be the last moment, instead feeding it some sense of calm in the hopes that it would be good for my dad. I stepped into the room tense. My heart was in pain.

"Hello," Aunt Janice said cheerfully as we entered the room.

I didn't know what to expect, but the smiles from Aunt Janice, my dad, and the nurse took me by surprise. The attending nurse wrote some notes on a chart, acting as if nothing big was happening, like it was an ordinary day. My fears began to melt away.

"Look what your dad can do," Aunt Janice nodded toward my dad's legs.

I looked at his feet. He lifted his right leg several inches.

"He was even doing small circles," the nurse pointed out.

He lifted his leg again and moved it in a small circle. Even though he winced in pain, he smiled, clearly filled with hope.

The *what if* washed away from me. Despite everything, he was still the same dad—strong, in control. He gave me that, a tremendous gift, and I clutched it like a child holding a teddy bear.

Just minutes later, the nurses wheeled him out of the room. I walked with him toward the double doors and told him, "I love you and I'll see you later."

"I love you and I'll see you later," I replied.

My mom leaned over and kissed him, repeating the same words. He rolled away through the double doors, which gently closed behind him as I caught one last glimpse of his gray-black hair.

THE MORNING LOOKED the same as it had the day before. Sunshine, warmth, stillness. Nothing moved . . . on the surface. Inside me, everything was moving, sorting itself out. I didn't need to rock. I didn't need to cry. All I had to do was wait.

The surgery was expected to take ten hours. We went home to wait. We planned on returning toward the end of the surgery unless a phone call came from the hospital.

No rocking, no crying, but not right. That sound— *a thousand cardboard boxes ripping at once*—haunted me. When I thought of that sound, the scene played out in my head from start to finish. I looked out the window over my dad's recliner at the tree, still balancing upright in its new unbalanced state. I worried it would fall at any time. I wanted it gone.

I noticed cars passing. Normally, cars sped down our street before slowing down a little to handle the gradual right turn past the woods next to our house. Now, they weren't speeding by. Instead, they slowed down and sometimes stopped. Faces peered out the window, staring at the tree and my mom's car. Their expressions ranged from shock to fear to amazement, and sadness, leaving me wondering. Were they simply passing by and surprised at what they saw, or had they heard something and wanted to check it out? For many, our house was the cute yellow older house with the well and the stone wall. To some, this was the Pitman house where Ron Pitman was raising his family. With each face that stopped and looked, I wondered what they knew.

I absolutely hate gawkers.

Ignoring the passing cars was my only option for coping. A few of my mom's friends visited, including Lynn, the mother of Tom, the first friend I ever had. We met in a play date when we were two. Our moms got us together often, even though we had different ideas of play. They called us the Bickertons. Tom wanted to sit and read to me about planets. I wanted to pretend we were butterflies. It frustrated Tom to no end when I wouldn't listen or didn't seem to care and I laughed at his impending tantrum. Despite this, we were buds, often sticking together in pre-school and at birthday parties. Kindergarten came and we were in different schools. We didn't see each other again until middle school and didn't reconnect as friends until high school, but when we did, the affection we had for each other as two-year-olds remained, minus the bickering.

Lynn was a counselor and unbeknown to me my mom felt it would be a good idea for her to come over and speak with me. My friends came over, occupying my time and my mind. I told them what happened and that my dad was going to be okay, explaining that he had been in great spirits when we last saw him.

Lynn sat at the kitchen table with my mom and a few other close friends. As much as I like Lynn, I sensed an agenda, one with the best intentions to help me, but one I did not want any part of.

I glanced at the kitchen clock as each passing hour trudged towards success. Each hour brought hope that my dad would have a better recovery, possibly regaining his ability to walk and saving his life. I wondered what was happening at every hour.

Hour one: *They're just getting started.*

Hour two: *They're probably accessing the damage, confirming or changing their plan as necessary.*

Hour four: *The team has found a rhythm, and it's working well.*

Hour five: *Halfway through.*

Hour seven: *So far so good—just a little longer.*

The hope spread, slowly eating away at *the thousand cardboard boxes*, gradually erasing my yesterday and returning life back to how it was. By the eighth hour, I began to experience what normal felt like again.

That's when the phone rang.

I heard it ring while sitting on the porch with my friends. It had been ringing a few times every hour, relief when it was discovered that the caller was a friend or family member. By the eighth hour, the ringing phone didn't faze me, until I heard the squeak of the screen door as Lynn stepped onto the porch and came toward me, concern in her eyes.

I stood up to face her. She turned me around and put her hands on my shoulders, calmly explaining to me that I had to go back to the hospital immediately.

Again, I didn't want to know. *Alive or dead?* All she could tell me was that my dad had a massive heart attack during the surgery.

ROCKING STARTED WHENEVER I sat down. It became automatic. Back and forth . . . back and forth . . . I looked like a drug addict going through withdrawal. Rocking stopped the tears, helped me breathe, kept my heart beating. I felt alone. No one else was rocking.

Back and forth . . . back and forth . . . gently easing the pain that was now building deep in my chest. My breath was shallow. Heartbreak.

I don't want to rock. I don't want to rock. I stopped, endured the pressure in my heart, but the force felt too great, like my soul was hanging on to my body by a thread. Rocking came back without me noticing, my soul's way of surviving, even when every desire of mine was to stop, to not look like a crazy person... or become one.

FOUR HOURS PASSED BEFORE finding out anything substantial. It started off with me and my mom sitting in a room, her friends closely by her side. My friend Andy had been on the porch when I got the news. He refused to leave; instead he followed us to the hospital and stayed with me. Aunt Janice came next. Then a few more close friends of my mom and dad. Then Uncle Bill, my dad's brother, and his girlfriend, Susan. My sister, Gayle, was stuck in California arranging a last-minute flight to Newark. Aunt Barbara, my dad's other sister, was on her way up from Virginia by car.

I rocked in front of all of them as we waited. Four hours of agony. Four hours of not knowing if my dad was alive or dead. We pleaded with nurses for information, but none had any to offer. I imagined the chaos in the operating room, doctors doing everything they could to keep him alive. I couldn't sit still, rocking back and forth, crying the entire time. I hadn't eaten in thirty hours. I hadn't slept in forty-six hours. My mom pleaded with me to eat, presenting a brownie someone had bought at the cafeteria. I didn't touch it; my stomach had completely turned off.

I needed help walking to the bathroom. My mom and Andy supported me on either side, my knees and back unable to hold me upright. Everything wanted to collapse.

After four hours, a doctor came with news. He explained that they had performed emergency heart surgery and it was successful. A gasp of relief escaped from all of us. My mom graciously grabbed the surgeon's hands, thanking him profusely. My dad was alive.

I stopped rocking. I had a few sips of water.

MY DAD WAS SURROUNDED by machines, all of them beeping a regularly irregular tune, recording every vital sign. I'd never seen him so helpless. Lying in his hospital bed with cold metal side rails, covered with white sheets and blankets, I watched him breathe gently in and out. That little movement in his chest, the only indication of life remaining. I ignored his swollen ears, nose, and hands. I dismissed the monitors measuring his pulse rate and blood pressure. All that mattered to me was his breathing, sometimes full, sometimes shallow, inhaling and exhaling.

The need to rock stopped and was replaced by a need to stop trekking down the path to crazy. I still couldn't eat. It was almost midnight. I presumed we would stay at the hospital to wait for the anesthesia to wear off and for my dad to slowly awaken, tired and sore, but smiling at us. I didn't want him to see me so weak, so broken, but I didn't know how to fix myself. After asking my mom, who was standing next to a nurse, if there was anyone I could talk to about what happened, a psychologist came within a half hour.

We sat in a small enclosed nook just on the other side of my dad's intensive care room. It was dark, lit only by a small lamp in the corner. Even without florescent lights and white walls, its tan walls and dorm room style chairs and coffee table appeared just as sterile as the other rooms. This is where the psychologist told me to write down everything that happened from start to finish in as much detail as possible, a first step towards separating the memories from myself, allowing the paper to hold them instead.

She found a small Steno pad with white paper and a black pen and left me alone in the room. I scribbled the details—the phone call, the porch, the sun, the wind, *a thousand cardboard boxes ripping at once*, my mom's car, the rain, the screams, the 9-1-1 call, my unconscious dad, the flashing lights, the lightning. I spewed as much as I could onto the pad, as much as I wanted to go back to a day and a half to remember in order to rid myself of the sounds and the images. After several pages, I stopped at the ER, believing that was all I needed to shed. I felt a little different; a weight still pressed me down but had lifted slightly from my shoulders. If I had been walking on a path, one direction being crazy and the other normal, at the very least I was now facing normal. I no longer felt I needed to force myself to breathe.

Satisfied about having taken my first step toward healing myself and making myself stronger for my dad, I flipped down the cover of the pad, secured the pen in the spiral binding, and stepped out into the florescent lights of the intensive care unit where I found my mom's brown leather purse on a chair just outside my dad's room. I tucked the pad into her outside pocket.

Just as I took my hands off my mom's purse, Tom, my Mr. Bickerton, appeared at my side. Andy had left after we heard that my dad had a successful surgery. I didn't expect any of my other friends to come. Seeing Tom surprised me. He shifted in discomfort as if he was battling with his own desire to be there for me as my friend and do whatever friends are supposed to do when one sees a tree fall on the other's dad. He admitted that he had no clue as to what to say. I was grateful that he was there at least.

I told Tom the surgery fixed the massive heart attack and that my dad was going to be okay, that this whole ordeal wasn't going to take down my dad, that he was stronger than this. I didn't tell Tom about my compulsive rocking or that I hadn't eaten or slept in over two days. I adamantly explained that everything was going to be okay, that I was fine, and that life would somehow be better because of this.

Tom shifted even more, looking around as if searching for the right thing to say or an exit route from this conversation. His body language said he wasn't convinced that my dad would be alright. All he could muster for the sake of helping and supporting me was one short question: "Are you sure?"

It hurt me, like a small nudge to the shoulder not intended to cause physical harm, but to send a message that says, "You are wrong," the possible first blow to an unintentional fight. I wanted to argue with Tom, to admonish him for doubting my dad's strength, so powerful that he had already beaten death twice and was still breathing. The white sheets and blankets were still rising and falling with every inhale and exhale. Life was still within him. I attempted to squash Tom's doubt as best as I could, smiling and repeating again and again that he would be fine.

Tom shifted even more with the nervous energy he couldn't contain. Obvious that he didn't know what else to do, he hugged me and told me he'd check on me the next day, avoiding eye contact with me as he said his goodbye. He found his exit route and walked toward it, more slowly than I expected, as if he didn't want to leave me but didn't know how to stay.

I left the intensive care unit to use the bathroom. It was the first time since returning to the hospital that I didn't need someone's help walking to the stall. I didn't need to go, there was nothing to eliminate, but I wanted a moment to myself outside of the unit. I sat on the toilet, searching for a moment of peace. I needed to breathe and quiet the thought that Tom had put in my head that my dad wasn't going to make it. My heart started to pound, my chest pains increased. As I sat inside the stall, I closed my eyes, tried to force a deep breath, and held it while clenching my fists, a relaxation technique I had learned when I was eight. I stayed like this for ten seconds. It had helped me as a child, but it didn't do much for me now. I tried it again, taking as deep a breath as possible, clenching my fists even tighter, and digging my nails into my palms. After another ten seconds, I released my breath and fists. Still, I felt no different. The thought was stuck with me, a sliver of doubt I could not release.

He's wrong. He doesn't know. Dad made it through the surgery. It's going to be okay. I stood, pulled up my pants, and pushed down the flusher handle even though the bowl gleamed with clear water, perhaps an unconscious attempt at flushing away the remaining uncertainty. I washed my hands three times . . . one last attempt to soothe myself before making my way back to the intensive care unit.

I took one last deep breath before opening the bathroom door and stepping back into an uncertain reality—one that I had been able to persuade myself was certain until Tom asked me that damned question: *Are you sure?* I opened the door and stepped out into the hallway, snaking my way through the short maze of turns back towards my dad's room. Passing through an intersection, I stopped as I unwittingly walked into a private moment between siblings. To my left at the end of the crossing hallway were Uncle Bill and Aunt Barbara, who had just arrived from Virginia. He was obviously catching her up. I couldn't hear them, but from thirty feet away with Uncle Bill's hands in his pockets and Aunt Barbara punching the air hard once with her hands while her bright blue eyes glistened with newly formed tears, I knew the essence of what was being said. They both looked toward me, immediately changing their posture to mask their emotion from me. On any other occasion, I would have run to them. Instead, I continued toward my dad's room, pretending that what I had just seen didn't happen.

As I entered the ICU, Aunt Janice walked out of my dad's room, tears streaming down her face. I had never seen her so sad. She met my eyes immediately. The doubt was no more. It was real. Aunt Janice embraced me and walked me to the tan sitting area where I had written everything down. We cried together, my tears acknowledging that I understood. She didn't need to tell me the news.

"How old were you when your dad died?" I asked her, remembering that my grandfather, my dad's dad, died at fifty-two from Hodgkin lymphoma.

"Seventeen," she said, through her tears, sharing that she knew my pain.

We cried together until it was time for everyone to gather and turn off the machines.

It took longer than I expected. I had always imagined that when someone was brain dead turning off life support would be like extinguishing an oil lamp, the flame becoming smaller and smaller until it disappeared into a puff of smoke. I knew my dad's death wouldn't be instantaneous, but I didn't think it would take over an hour and a half.

Gayle was probably flying over the Midwest at that time, possibly over where my dad was born in Indiana. She was the only one missing in the room. The rest of us stayed with him as his life came to its conclusion: me and my mom to his right, with my aunts, uncles, and grandmother circling the foot of the bed and Uncle Bill to his left. Machines still beeped, tracking every heartbeat, every last bit of life. They slowed and came back, like he was hovering between being alive and dead. Alive and dead ... back and forth. The dozen times that the beeping was regular, almost healthy, I wondered if he was fighting. I knew he didn't want to leave us. There was too much left to do. Graduations. Weddings. Grandkids. Fishing trips. Golf outings. Holidays. Growing old with my mom. He had wanted to celebrate their thirtieth wedding anniversary the next month.

I looked at the clock hanging on the wall. It read 3:15 am. Over an hour of us watching him pass on, still clinging to life. Everyone was crying as my dad lay in his bed stuck between life and death, as if he was unsure what to do. He had to leave us, but how could he with all of us crying?

I leaned toward him and whispered, "Just go. It's going to be okay." Five minutes later, the beeping slowed down considerably, but still continued. My mom took his hand and gave him one last squeeze and then left the room. I followed her, the rest of my family slowly stepping out behind me. Uncle Bill came out last.

AT HOME, THE RISING SUN lightened the night sky. I wanted to sleep, but wasn't sure I knew how to fall asleep anymore, how to give in to relaxation and allow my body to rest. My mind wouldn't stop—*a thousand cardboard boxes*, the rain, the wind, the thunder, the flashing lights, the rocking, the hospital, the broken eye glasses, the sleepless night, the relief, the last words, the phone call, the ICU, the swollen ears, the rising and falling of my dad's chest, the time. So many details flashed through my thoughts, not wanting to let go.

Could I forget this? No. The bigger question—did I want to forget this? No, I didn't. Forgetting would mean letting go of another part of my dad, a bad part, but another thing I didn't want to lose. I wanted the memories to slow down, to tuck themselves into a corner of my brain where I could access them if I wanted. Instead, everything played out over and over again on repeat. I didn't know how to stop it, but hoped that sleep would help.

But sleep seemed scary. Dreams could turn into nightmares with more images and sounds to haunt me. There was no chance I could sleep in my own bed with the tree looming unbalanced in the front yard. I asked Aunt Barbara if she would sit in the living room and watch me sleep. She sat on the uncomfortable vintage armchair with the cream and rust pattern with dark-stained wooden arms. The other option she couldn't bring herself to sit on—the big, cushy, soft, blue Ethan Allen armchair, the one unspokenly reserved for my dad when we opened Christmas presents or sat in the living room together enjoying a roaring fire he had built in the antique iron wood-burning fireplace.

I grabbed a hand-knit patchwork blanket made by my great-grandmother from a stack of family-made blankets that were neatly folded and stacked in the built-in book shelves, kicked off my flip flops, and lay down on the dark green couch, resting my head on a matching rust-colored throw pillow. Before closing my eyes, I looked at Aunt Barbara. She wasn't crying, the one family member who knew how to cry better than anyone else. Sappy greeting cards made her weep, even if they weren't hers. When the Denville EMT volunteers stopped in front of our house every Christmas Eve and handed out stockings filled with candy to all the neighborhood children, she choked out a thank you through tears every single time. She would cry with guilt at any mention of the time when she was a kid and out of jealousy purposely broke Aunt Janice's pink umbrella over her knee—the one my dad gave to her for Christmas and had "Janice" beautifully written on the fabric—even after decades of saying she was sorry. I remembered her in the hall-way with Uncle Bill when I came out of the bathroom. From a distance, I knew she had been balling. Now, she seemed to tuck away her grief. Watching me was her way of helping me get away from crazy.

I closed my eyes. The sun streamed more and more light into the living room. My racing mind slowed down little by little the longer I stayed still. My breath was shallow. My heart hurt. Drifting off seemed impossible, like I would never be able to do it again. I craved sleep, wanting that wonderful deep, quiet sleep that leaves you wondering how it's possible to achieve that level of peace and escape from every bad thing that has ever happened in one's life. Even with Aunt Barbara watching me, I couldn't reach it, instead lying still for over an hour as morning grew brighter and brighter.

Through the gentle breeze that wafted from the porch through the screen door passed the dining room and in toward my head on the couch, I heard car doors closing. Gayle was home. Uncle Bill had gone and picked her up at Newark Airport. I didn't have it in me to get up and greet her. My love for my older sister was overpowered by my extreme desire to find the tiniest bit of inner quiet. I kept my eyes shut as Aunt Barbara told me that Gayle was home, pretending to sleep so that I could be left alone. Then I heard Gayle come in through the screen door and walk toward me through the dining room, pass me in the living room without stopping, make her way around the corner, and go down the hall to my mom and dad's bedroom. It was only when I heard Gayle's sobs that I realized my mom had been lying alone in her bed since we came home, maybe trying to find the same quiet I was searching for. As Gayle wept for many minutes, I let my grief go for a moment, allowing my sister to cry for both of us. It was only then that I finally found a peace for twenty minutes before the sun's brightness wouldn't allow me to sleep anymore.

VISITORS CAME . . . LOTS OF THEM. Many I expected: close family friends, my friends. Some I didn't know. I endured awkward greetings from people I hadn't seen in ages, who seemed on the periphery of our family's life. Some who hadn't been to our house in over a decade were noting the lovely "new" wallpaper in the dining room, which had been put up years before, or our "new" kitchen, which my mom and dad remodeled so long ago that it was in need of another makeover. Now, they expressed their grief as if they couldn't imagine us going through this loss without them. I wondered where they were before. I didn't want to share.

Not that I didn't appreciate the kind words everyone offered about my dad, as well as the dozens of sympathy cards that included notes of how positively he had touched their lives. I understood that my dad was a very well-respected person in our community. At the same time, the outpouring was overwhelming. The window looking into my dad's life was bigger than I ever expected. So many cards came from people I had never met. To me, he was my dad and his family was his world. I wanted to grieve only within that realm.

Also, with each encounter my back stiffened up with tremendous tension in the hopes that I wouldn't start naturally rocking. I didn't want anyone to think I was crazy. It took all of my energy to stay still. I'd never felt so out-of-control of my body in my life.

The visitors all brought sandwiches, pasta, or desserts, large catering-type platters of food. Every inch of countertop had something to offer, eventually spreading to the butcher block kitchen table. We could have opened a pop-up deli. Ham. Swiss. Turkey. American cheese. Mustards. Mayo. Pickles. Coleslaw. Olives. The kitchen smelled of salted meats among the two trays of lasagna, penne vodka, and eggplant parmesan. The brownies, cookies, cake, and pie found the last unoccupied spot on the butcher block table, perhaps for easier access as people gathered around. It became comical when through the TV room window I saw my friend Jordan getting out of his car and opening the passenger seat, taking out the largest platter of cold cuts and two loaves of bread, knowing there was not a square inch of space left to set down any more food. Less than half of everything fit in our refrigerator. My mom asked Aunt Barbara to call the neighbors and see if they would take some of our spread.

Aunt Barbara acted as the receptionist for the day. The phone rang constantly. She found an unused legal pad in my dad's desk and wrote down every message. I didn't take any phone calls and my mom only spoke to family members or the funeral home. I don't recall a single moment during the day where Aunt

PEACE WITH TREES

Barbara's hand was not holding the phone to her left ear as she took notes on the legal pad. By the end of the day, there were several pages of messages, each note likely offering condolences and well wishes, but feeling more and more like people peering in. I grew tired of hearing the phone ring.

The tree still teetered, drawing attention. As I watched out the TV room windows, more cars slowed down, wanting to take a peek at it. Some stopped abruptly and I saw more surprised faces of people wondering what had happened. Others seemed to slow down gradually, as if purposely driving by to get a glimpse, to see the aftermath. Word spread. More phone calls, more visitors, more slowing cars. More gawkers.

I picked at the food, not eating enough to say I had a meal. Each bite felt like a test to my stomach, seeing if the food would stay down and settle in. Bites stayed down, but nothing felt comfortable, not even from the plethora of once yummy options that were available.

Chest pains remained. My back was tight and sore. Exhausted, I still didn't know how to sleep. I needed help breaking the cycle of my sleeplessness. "Do you think I could maybe get some sort of sleeping pill for tonight?" I asked my mom.

Mom said she'd contact the pediatrician, the one I'd had since birth and had outgrown, but continued to see, never yet having had the opportunity to find an adult doctor. Relief washed over me knowing that I might actually sleep that night, something I hadn't done in over fifty hours.

More of my friends came. We gathered in the living room. They all knew the story, most having heard it from Kristine, who often acted as the center of our social group. Her role had evolved organically since her house was the most centrally located and her parents didn't care if their house became our hangout spot. They never locked their door. If you didn't get a phone call with plans for Saturday night, a safe bet was to show up at Kristine's house, even if she wasn't home. Eventually, everyone would end up there and stay late into the night. Mainly for that reason alone, Kristine always knew what was going on. Now was no exception. Perhaps that was also why she was the first person I had called. She sat in the soft blue Ethan Allen chair.

My friends talked about anything except what happened while I listened. I didn't want to talk at all. Instead, I asked Jordan, the bringer of a large platter of cold cuts, who was now sitting next to me on the green couch, if he wouldn't mind if I lay down and rested my head on his leg. I was too exhausted to sit up and it felt awkward to ask any of my friends if they could hold me, so resting my head on Jordan's thigh seemed like the least crazy option.

An hour or so into their visit, all at once my dad's golf buddies came along with their wives, who were carrying more platters of food, as if they planned on coming together. The women were as I'd always seen them at the country club: made up, carrying designer handbags, and wearing what looked like outfits they'd just picked up that day. Their sparkling jewelry and watches could have been mistaken as costume accessories, given their size, but I knew the pieces were all real. My mom's posture shot straight up once they arrived. My friends and I were quickly banished from the living room so the country club friends could gather around my mother there. We made our way to the breezeway, grabbing some food as we passed through the kitchen.

After returning from the bathroom, Tom had made his way to the living room to discover that not only were there different people sitting on the couch and armchairs, but the vibe had drastically changed as well. "It's like a fine cocktail party in there," he noted as he stepped into the breezeway. "Who are those people?"

"They're my dad's golfing buddies," I answered.

"Really? They're friends of your dad's?" he asked.

"Yeah."

"I mean . . . ," he searched. "I don't know how to put it . . . but it's weird in there. It doesn't look like they're grieving somebody."

I had to see for myself. I got up and went through the kitchen to the dining room. Before even setting foot into the living room, I heard light laughter, the kind you hear after someone tells a funny story about leaving the house having put eye shadow on one eye or forgetting to pack dress shoes and having to wear tennis sneakers with a suit for an event immediately after a round of golf. I wanted to walk in and remind everyone why they were visiting, that this wasn't a cocktail party, but my mom sat poised among the group on a dining room chair she had brought in for extra seating, listening to everyone else talk and receiving whatever kind of support this crew gave. Clearly, this was for her and no one else. I couldn't understand. The energy that wafted out of the living room didn't match the rest of the house.

I got halfway into the dining room before I turned around to go back to my friends. The energy pushed me back, as if the room shouted out to anyone else in the house, "This is how we're dealing with this and that's okay." I had nothing in me to disagree, just enough to agree with Tom that it was weird in there.

Aunt Janice and Aunt Barbara sat in the kitchen. "Susie, who are those people in the living room?" Aunt Barbara asked.

"They're the country club friends. My dad played golf with the guys."

"I thought you and your friends were in the living room," Gayle said as she came into the kitchen. "I came downstairs and rounded the corner, not expecting to walk into what looked like high tea at nearly dinnertime. It's kind of weird in there."

I was glad I wasn't alone in my feelings.

IT WAS VERY DARK OUTSIDE by the time all the visitors left. We sat around the butcher block table and picked out clothes for my dad. My mom brought out two suits, two shirts, two ties, and two pairs of leather dress shoes for us to select. We settled on the gray suit, white shirt, and gray and red tie, a combination he often chose and looked great in. After we made our decision, my mom glanced down and sighed at what she saw.

"*Awww*, look everyone."

We looked down and saw Mickey, his eyes wet, resting his cheek on the side of my dad's black leather shoes, the part that normally my dad would slip his foot into.

AUNT BARBARA STAYED with us. She slept in the guest room just down the hall from my room, from my perspective the most vulnerable room in the house. She didn't seem to have much concern as her bag was already opened on the luggage stand against the wall, just like it always was when she stayed over.

I was determined to sleep well, even though I was wide awake still thinking about *a thousand cardboard boxes*. Whenever I was alone with my thoughts, the sounds and images repeated. Knowing Aunt Barbara was nearby, I chose to be brave and sleep in my own bed, forcing myself to step further away from crazy, from being too scared of my own room. I changed into sweat shorts and a tee-shirt and noticed the pre-scription bottle next to a glass of water on the wood nightstand beside my white iron bed. It sat there waiting for me to take it, to aid me into a wonderfully deep sleep without me needing to try. Relief relaxed my tense upper body. Any fears of forgetting how to sleep would be swept away by these pills. I wondered what this magic pill was called, this easy solution to softening my thoughts for one night of deep, unclut-tered sleep. Curious, I picked up the bottle and read the name of the medication.

Xanax.

I didn't know anything about Xanax, but even so, I didn't want it. I looked all over the bottle—nothing said Xanax would help me sleep. I knew these weren't sleeping pills. Feeling frustrated and angry that I didn't get what I asked, I went downstairs into the kitchen where I found my mom, Gayle, and Aunt Barbara sitting at the butcher block table.

"This isn't what I asked for," I announced as I entered, holding up the orange prescription bottle.

Three faces looked back at me. "What do you mean?" my mom asked.

"I asked for a sleeping pill. This isn't a sleeping pill," I said authoritatively, not knowing if it was true.

My mom hesitated but gave in. "You're right," she said, "it isn't a sleeping pill. It's for anxiety."

A label I didn't want: *anxiety*. I hated that it was assumed I had it even though a doctor hadn't seen me. I had stopped myself from rocking. I was doing everything I could to get away from any mental disorder. I didn't want that diagnosis or any that suggested I was not okay or that I was not going to be okay.

"But I don't have anxiety," I reasoned. "I just need help sleeping."

An elephant walked into the room.

Aunt Barbara treaded carefully. "They're going to help you sleep tonight . . . ," she started to say.

"No they won't," I interrupted. "They're for anxiety!"

"Susie, they're not just for anxiety," my mom explained. "They can also help with sleep."

"But aren't they addicting?" I asked, searching for another reason to validate that I should not take them.

"You're not going to get addicted," my mom assured me. "The doctor only prescribed three pills."

"Fine," I said through clenched teeth as I stormed out and stomped back upstairs to my room.

Still, what my mom said stuck with me: *They can also help with sleep.* Dreading another night of not remembering how to sleep, I sat on the edge of the bed and looked at the bottle before pushing down and twisting the cap until I heard a small pop. At the bottom lay three pills, forming an innocent triangle. They looked safe, sitting in a bottle much bigger than they needed. I tilted the bottle, letting one small pill slide into my palm.

You better help me sleep tonight. I brought my palm to my mouth and felt the pill sitting on my tongue. I washed it down with a swig of room-temperature water. It went down with no effort. I put the cap back on the bottle, twisting it until it locked into place.

I climbed into bed, tucking myself under the sheet and quilt—the same bedding that had enveloped me in sleep since I outgrew my crib, back when sleep was easy. Resting my head on my pillow, I gazed out the window at the tops of the trees silhouetted against the night sky, the same view that put me to sleep every night since I could remember. Once beautiful to me, it now felt as if it had betrayed me. I turned my back to the window, curling into the fetal position and trying not to cry. I stared at the clock: 10:05 pm. Wide awake. I closed my eyes, hoping it would help the pill. Instead, my mind couldn't escape my dad, *a thousand cardboard boxes*, the hospital, the visitors today, the slowing cars passing our house. I tried thinking of other things, avoiding the beach, believing that same poetic story would keep me up the entire night like it had perfectly done two nights before. Nothing else came to mind. I looked around my room, staring at all the familiar things—my birds-eye maple dresser with my wooden jewelry boxes reflecting against the mirror, the cream wallpaper with the tiny yellow and peach flowers that blossomed on thin, green, curly stems, the antique quilt with dozens of differently patterned fabrics sewn together to form flowers against a white background.

I looked at the clock: 11:30 pm. I knew this wasn't going to work. I spent the rest of the night lying in darkness under that quilt, doing nothing and everything to not think about *a thousand cardboard boxes* and flashing lights, avoiding looking out the window.

I LAY IN BED A LONG TIME, avoiding the day. I presumed there would be more visitors, more food, and more slowing cars. I hadn't slept, but being horizontal all night at least released some of my fatigue and stirred a slight appetite. Once it grew large enough for me to get excited about eating, I got up and made my way downstairs to the kitchen. I saw Gayle sitting at the butcher block table reading a newspaper. Two other papers were strewn about, their headlines facing up.

"Denville Lawyer Dies of Injuries Suffered During Violent Storm: Tree branch fell on former school board president" . . . *The Daily Record*.

"Bad Storm Claims the Life of Ron Pitman, 53" . . . *The Citizen*.

"Three Lives Collide with a Violent Storm" . . . *The Star Ledger* let everyone know my dad was not alone.

Front page news, not completely shocking. He was an attorney who specialized in real estate transactions and small business formations for over twenty years at a small firm in downtown Denville where he was the senior partner. Lots of people knew him. Throughout my childhood, nearly every teacher or coach I ever had acknowledged to me that they knew my dad and that he had done excellent work for them. Now he was known as the guy who was hit by the tree.

"You're not going to like what they said in this one article," Gayle cautioned me as she pointed to *The Star Ledger*.

"What do you mean?" I asked.

"They got the story wrong."

She showed me. "His wife, Sally, heard the tree snap, looked out the window and called 9-1-1 before running outside to help him." None of us had spoken to any press.

"Here too," she added.

The Citizen: "The 9-1-1 call from Pitman's wife Sally was made at 5:08 pm. . . ." No, she didn't.

Other details . . . "Pitman awoke when the rescue squad arrived, but was disoriented and didn't know which day it was, police said . . ." a detail I wished nobody knew.

"He was hit on the head and back . . ." No, he wasn't.

I was too exhausted to care that the stories were wrong.

Among the untruths were beautiful words: "'Nobody can believe it,' Vito Bianco, Denville's council president, said of Pitman's death. 'If you needed to raise money for something, he was always there. He was always an active, good neighbor in the community.'"

"'He's been an important leader in our community for over twenty years,' said former Mayor Jim Dyer. 'He served in many different capacities. He brought a sense of stability to our community and was always good natured and respected.'"

WE CHOSE A CLOSED CASKET, even though the swelling had gone down and my dad looked significantly better. The funeral director allowed us to view him one last time before preparing him for the closed casket. Another one-last-time to add to the list of other last-times, such as the last Yankee game, last time getting the mail, last words.

Our last car ride together had proved more significant than I expected. My dad came home from playing golf with his usual foursome when he had what had seemed to him to be a brilliant and exciting idea. "Susie, let's go shopping!" he'd exclaimed.

The only other time I had gone shopping with my dad was when it was his job to keep me out of the house for a few hours, so my mom could prepare for a family surprise party for my seventeenth birthday. Our assignment was to find snow boots, something my mom expected would take hours since I was notoriously picky when it came to buying anything. To my dad's surprise, I found the perfect boots on the first display in the first store we visited. My dad suggested we keep shopping, but I didn't pick up on the opportunity. Instead, I was tired, having taken the PSAT that morning after waking up with a stomach ache. I wanted to go home and take a nap, but my dad insisted on walking around the mall for two hours. Had I had more energy and picked up on my dad's enthusiasm for buying me clothes I didn't need, my closet could have been filled with sweaters from Benetton, blazers from the Limited, and a few pairs of jeans and tee-shirts from Gap.

This last shopping excursion the morning before the tree ripped apart wasn't for anything exciting. I had mentioned to my mom and dad that I was going to buy toiletries and cleaning supplies once I got up to Syracuse, so I didn't have to fit them into my car with everything else. "I'd rather get those things after I move into my apartment at college," I said reasonably.

He didn't let up. "Come on, let's get those things now."

I gave in, realizing that for whatever reason it would make my dad really happy. I grabbed my purse and we walked out the screen door onto the porch that connected to the garage. My dad pushed the garage door opener as I got into the front seat of his Cadillac. Even though my dad had his dream car for nearly a year, it still smelled like new car. My dad opened the driver's side door and got in. He put the car in reverse, but after only backing out a few feet, he abruptly put the car in park, turned off the engine, and opened his door.

"I'll be right back," he said.

I sat there shocked at how agile my very tall and overweight dad appeared jumping out of the car, wondering what was so important for this mundane trip to the store. Minutes later, he came back and hit the button to open the trunk. I noticed a CD in his hand, not just any CD, but the one I had given to him for his fifty-third birthday, which had been only two weeks before: Bob Carlyle's *Butterfly Kisses*. He hadn't listened to the CD. It had been sitting by the stereo in the living room with the plastic wrap still around it.

For whatever reason, my dad had decided to get out of the car, go back into the house, find the CD, remove the nearly impossible-to-remove plastic wrapping along with the even-more-impossible-to-remove clear sticker that ran along the top edge of the case, come back to the car with the CD, and open the trunk to access the CD changer, a newer feature in cars that manufacturers felt it best to tuck deep inside the trunk in order to preserve space. My dad usually kept the same CDs in the changer because it was such a pain to remove them.

As we drove up our street to take the back roads on that perfectly sunny early afternoon, my dad remained quiet for the first half of the title song "Butterfly Kisses." I looked over at him every once in a while to see if he was getting it. He had a slight smile while driving. A tiny tear formed at the corner of his eye, but didn't drop. We never talked about the meaning of the lyrics, but I knew he was getting it.

I have not been able to listen to that song since.

I HAD NOTHING TO WEAR. I needed two outfits: one for the viewing and one for the funeral. Even though the staff at the funeral home knew this would be a "big one," it was easy for my mom to decide to have two long wakes in one day rather than draw out the formalities over two days. I had a long black dress with tiny white flowers that I reserved for the funeral. The only other dress that fit me and was conservative enough for the wake was a dress I got years before. I couldn't remember why I got it in the first place. It was a long, cream-colored dress with roses, lace, pleats, and a corset design at the waist, reminiscent of the Laura Ashley-style dresses that had been popular when I was younger, but now looked like something an eight-year-old would wear. Everything about that dress was ridiculous, but my mom said she loved it and thought it would be appropriate to wear.

I felt uncomfortable the second I put the dress on, but with only an hour before we had to leave, I told myself no one would care about what I wore. The minute we arrived at the funeral home, I wished I had worn the other black dress, even though that would have meant wearing it two days in a row.

My mom stood in the middle of the room and greeted every single person that came. A line stretched all the way to the door. I sat in a chair near the casket and watched. I didn't know how my mom could stand there, perfectly poised, holding everyone's hand as they expressed their condolences. I wanted to curl up in a ball and escape the crowd. Lots of faces . . . some familiar . . . more I didn't recognize, and some who resembled the first responders who had been at the scene of the accident. I wondered, *Of*

these faces, who was a client of Dad's? Who gave the false
story to the newspaper? Who here is a distant connection
that none of us expected to arrive? Only those I knew
came up to me, giving me a momentary escape from
any obligation I felt to thank people for coming, even
though I hardly acted on that obligation. Thankfully
my mom appeared to be handling that responsibility
without needing any help from me or Gayle.

I wanted to rock, but I didn't want anyone to see
me rock. My back stiffened as I sat. Rocking often
started without me noticing, so I sat as upright as I
could. The room grew louder as it filled with people.
The humid air thickened. That along with the polyes-
ter in my dress made me sweat. I couldn't wait to go
home and change into my shorts and a tee-shirt.

Some people asked me questions. They were few
and far between, but noted. I didn't say much, except
I did explain that most of the newspapers got the
story wrong. I hated that there was a story. I wanted
people to look at the photos we had displayed on
poster boards placed throughout the room. Photos of
my dad fishing, at birthday parties, playing whiffle
ball, on the beach, sleeping in the recliner with

Mickey on his lap . . . That's how I wanted him re-membered—not as the guy who was hit by a tree.

Both wakes ran longer than expected. Afterward, my mom told me the funeral home director discretely asked her to help move the line along. We knew it stretched to the door, but we didn't know that be-cause it was raining traffic built up as people waited in their cars for their turn to enter. By the time it was over, the energy I had contained to keep from crying and rocking in front of everyone drained me.

That night, I slept without effort.

IN THE LIMOUSINE, I SAT next to my mom and across from Uncle Bill. My whole family was together, dressed up, sitting in silence and staring out the win-dow at another beautifully still summer day. Disbelief is what I felt. Despite the wonderful sleep I got the night before, this wasn't a nightmare. This was real. I couldn't believe I was actually going to the funeral for my dad.

The route was all too familiar. It was the same one I had taken nearly every day of my childhood to get to school, dance classes, softball games, and whatever other activities I had going on in Denville. Everything looked the same, but nothing felt the same. Passing by my dad's law firm downtown, I saw his name on the door. I wished he was sitting at his large wooden desk, wearing a white shirt and striped tie, reading a contract, his jacket neatly hung in his closet ready for the meeting he had scheduled later that day.

Approaching the church, cars lined the street. I knew it would be packed. I dreaded the crowd. Everyone was already seated or standing in the back as we entered. I'd never seen it that full. I kept my gaze down, avoiding eye contact. We sat in the front two pews.

I elected to give a eulogy, knowing that this would be my only opportunity ever to ensure that people got to know my dad as he really was and not just as the guy hit by a tree. The night before, I thought about what life lessons he taught me. We had only just begun having those adult conversations. That transition from parent/child relationship to friendship had only started a year before. I badly wanted more of that.

"There's several things I learned from my dad," I started, surprised at how normal my voice sounded. I approached it as one last gift to my dad, hoping that the major lessons he taught me would inspire others to approach life in a similar way and that the impact of his short time on this planet would continue. I looked up and saw Jordan, the bearer of the platter of cold cuts and two loaves of bread, sitting with several of my friends. More familiar faces dotted the crowd. Most of them were unfamiliar. Just like I had wondered during the wake, as I spoke I wondered again . . . *How did they know him?* I thought I knew everyone close in my dad's life.

". . . and for my twenty years, I could not have asked for a better dad."

POLICE ESCORTED THE procession to the cemetery a half hour away. Looking out the window of the limousine, I saw police cars blocking side streets the entire way. Flags at town hall flew at half-staff, even though my dad was not a public servant. People crowded around the gravesite, more than I wanted because I didn't know many of them.

I wished it was only me and my family, like it had been in the ICU when we watched him pass. I wanted my mom, Gayle, Gram, my aunts, uncles, and cousins to have this final moment, unwatched in peace. The day continued to be beautifully still, the sunshine bringing even more vibrancy to the flowers that surrounded his casket, the only thing I could take in. Soon he'd be placed in the ground. I kept my focus on the flowers, blocking out the mass of unfamiliar faces as best as I could.

Alive or dead. Crying, rocking, not eating, not sleeping. *A thousand cardboard boxes ripping at once.* Gawkers driving by our house and coming to the hospital, many of them now at the cemetery. Many were supposed to be there, but I wondered why those I did not recognize had come.

We weren't even the last ones to leave.

Off

SILENCE. THE ACTIVITY WENT AWAY as swiftly as if someone had hit the light switch. Cars no longer slowed down once the tree and my mom's car were cleared. The phone didn't ring. People didn't come with food. The mailman stopped delivering boxes of sympathy cards. I wondered, *Now what?*

Without hesitation, I decided to take the semester off, not wanting to face what I knew would be a difficult semester. On top of learning how to sleep again and wondering how I was ever going to quiet the noise from *a thousand cardboard boxes*, let alone how I would even manage the responsibilities of classes and papers, what was waiting for me back at college was a redo of the most important test of my college career. At the end of my spring semester, I had failed my sophomore evaluation. Nearly half of my class failed, so I wasn't alone, but it was a big deal to me. I was an acting student. The two-minute scene that was required for the evaluation was the key that unlocked a bachelor's degree in fine arts, the one that signified that the department believed in that student and felt the student would make it in the entertainment industry. Failing didn't mean you were toast. However, it was highly encouraged for students who failed to choose the Bachelor of Science route, a path that not only felt like bullshit to me, but actually resulted in a B.S. This was also known in the acting community at school as the "fallback plan." My second chance to undergo evaluation was to be at the end of the fall semester my junior year. I wanted to pass, but nothing in me wanted to face that test. I stayed home.

I focused my energy on keeping the need to cry below the surface, enough so that it wouldn't spill over. My dad and the tree occupied my mind constantly. I didn't know if I would ever be able to get away from it.

But I tried, literally. My mom and dad had reserved a room at one of the vintage motels in Wildwood Crest, a place that Aunt Barbara discovered as a good shore spot for Aunt Janice and Uncle Jeff's family vacations. My mom still had the reservation and she convinced Gayle to stay in New Jersey and go down the Shore. I had never been to Wildwood Crest, but knowing that I was going to sit in a beach chair and dig my toes into the sand and swim in the ocean made me welcome a change from mentally numbing myself to stop thinking of *a thousand cardboard boxes*.

My familiar shore spot was Surf City on Long Beach Island. My dad's grandfather had owned a house on the island in Beach Haven, and so he had spent summers there swimming, fishing, crabbing, searching the sand with a metal detector, and making memories with his family. Space was limited in the tiny Cape Cod-style house, the top floor occupied only by beds, including a short bed that had been built into a nook in order to create as many sleeping spaces as possible. I heard stories of dinner times when a bowl of spaghetti was passed with many only getting two or three strands of pasta because not enough was cooked for the number of people who showed up to eat. My dad, Uncle Bill, Aunt Barbara, and their cousins would go out afterward, grabbing pizza at Jetstream, the dive down the street, leaving Aunt Janice behind because she was little.

My mom had put up with the crowded scene from the time when she first began to date my dad until they got married and had Gayle. It was then she insisted that they rent a separate house on the island. Eventually, they settled on an oceanfront house, the top floor of a duplex in Surf City. For two weeks every July of my childhood until the year before my dad passed, we spent our annual vacation at that house. It had dark wooden paneling and only one bathroom. There was no air conditioning and when a west wind came off the mainland, it brought hot air and bugs. The house sat on pilings and the only access to the unit was the deck steps, which shook and splintered a little more every year. Inside was a large wooden couch with brown and tan plaid cushions and two matching armchairs. The wood on the furniture was caked with the grimy residue of salt air and suntan lotion, which left a film on you when you would rest an elbow or hand on it. Behind the one armchair in the living room hung a large painting of a ship in turbulent waters. In the corner hung a coconut decorated to look like a head. Tacky shell knickknacks sat on every surface. There was no TV.

On the surface, nothing seemed special about this house, but nearly every special moment I had with my family happened there. There is where we'd wake up to the sounds of waves crashing. There is where we'd eat elephant ears for breakfast, a pastry I've only ever found at the bakery a block away. There is where we'd put on SPF 8 suntan lotion before heading down the long flight of wooden stairs and around and over the dune to the beach for the day, beach chair, towel, and yellow Styrofoam surfboard in hand.

On that beach, I learned how to ride waves on that Styrofoam surf board. My dad and Uncle Bill would push me and Gayle for hours. We were the furthest ones out at the line where only the biggest and best waves broke, giving us the longest ride possible. My dad and Uncle Bill each held the nose of the board facing the ocean while Gayle and I waited on top. They were on the lookout, waiting for the perfect wave.

"This is a good one," my dad would signal. "Hold on!" The next thing I knew, my dad would take a deep breath and dive under, holding the nose of the board and flinging it over his head, then pushing the tail with his hand, propelling me with the wave all the way to the sand. My dad and Uncle Bill did this for hours, sending me and Gayle flying on waves faster and longer than every other kid. Each ride would take me all the way to the sand, salt water misting my face as my heart raced with excitement.

"Dad?" I called once after paddling back.

"What?"

"This is the best day ever."

My dad smiled brightly. "You're right. This is the best day ever."

Those days were gone once we outgrew the Styrofoam surfboards, replaced by bobbing in the water and jumping waves. Then, once Gayle and I entered adulthood and our time was taken by summer jobs, they were gone altogether. A year before the tree fell we took our last family vacation in Surf City.

None of this came to mind before my mom, Gayle, and I were driving down to Wildwood Crest. It was only until I was sitting on a beach chair, digging my toes into the sand and staring out toward the water that the memories flooded back. Styrofoam surf boards were now replaced by boogie boards that kids clutched as they looked over their shoulders for the perfect wave, jumping aboard at the wrong time or for the wrong wave, their ride less than a second long. Those were the types of kids that Gayle and I rode past fifteen years earlier. Looking out at the surf break, I saw the four of us out there, waiting for the big one. I would have given anything to do that again.

I'd never been to Wildwood Crest with my dad, but the Shore is the Shore. Reminders of him were everywhere. The sand. The beach chairs. The seagulls. The sun. The breeze. The airplane banners. The boats. The ice cream truck bell. The smell of suntan lotion. The Jersey Shore was his favorite place. Every moment I thought of him.

But I didn't cry constantly. I missed him, but the reminders brought me comfort. These things were still here. He would never be forgotten, nor would I only remember him with *a thousand cardboard boxes*.

ONE THING OUT OF CHARACTER happened on that trip. We were crabbing in the bay, not having much luck. Of the four traps Aunt Janice brought, many of which were so old it's possible my dad used them decades ago, we caught six crabs, hardly a bounty for our large group. While walking on the dirty wooden pier back to the car, I stepped on a bent, rusty, three-inch nail, which twisted in such a way that it punctured the inside of my foot. It was hardly a gash, it didn't bleed, but its small pinch made me scream and sink to the pier in a heap of hysterics over needing a tetanus shot.

I couldn't believe my reaction, but I also could not stop crying. I felt like the nail had pierced a bubble that contained my emotions. Beforehand, I didn't even know I had a bubble.

GAYLE FLEW BACK TO CALIFORNIA the day after we returned from Wildwood Crest. More silence. More beautiful days. My friends were all back at college. The deli that was our kitchen was mostly empty now. My mom boxed and stored the sympathy cards.

The only evidence of our deep loss was what no longer remained and my racing thoughts.

A thousand cardboard boxes . . . a sound I could think of in an instant. The thought of it brought everything back to the beginning, back to standing on the porch on the day that went from beautiful to sideways. I tried to think of other things, but it crept back now and then. One evening, while sitting on the couch with Mickey on my lap watching the Yankee game, I reminded myself that I was supposed to be at Syracuse University watching a musical, but *a thousand cardboard boxes* was why I was home.

Going out for pizza with my mom to the place we'd gone to every Friday for several years, all I thought about was my craving for the fried mushrooms, until the owner asked us where the "big guy" was . . . *a thousand cardboard boxes*. After my mom explained he had passed, he asked if he was the guy who was hit by a tree. *A thousand cardboard boxes*.

Driving past my dad's law firm in Denville, seeing his name on the door. *A thousand cardboard boxes*.

Returning to a part-time job I'd had at a clothing store, listening to customers' creative excuses for why they needed their money back after they altered their garments too small or ripped their grass-stained jeans so easily while playing what was obviously not touch football, their problems seemed minuscule against *a thousand cardboard boxes*.

Entering the kitchen early one morning less than two weeks after the tree fell, my mom's wet eyes greeted me. "Susie, I have some really bad news for you," she cautioned.

A thousand cardboard boxes.

What now . . . ? I thought.

"Princess Diana was killed in a car accident in Paris last night."

William and Harry came to mind immediately. So much younger than me, now facing a loss I knew too well and on a stage much larger than mine. Gawkers took her life whereas for me they had only peered in on our family tragedy from what felt like too close a distance. Different circumstances and different worlds to be sure, but that morning waking up to the news every part of me felt like I knew what those boys were feeling.

Walking in a parking lot from my car to the store, a large brown vintage car started to back up just as I was behind it. I screamed and slapped my hand on the trunk. The red brake lights immediately flashed, bringing the car to a stop. Rather than continuing on, I brought my foot up with the intention of slamming it into the chrome fender, wanting to punish the driver, to punctuate how terrible it would have been if he had hit me. *A thousand cardboard boxes*. I stopped myself just as I was about to kick my leg down, my conscience saving me. Intense anger followed, at the driver, at myself, at the tree, at the world. It stayed with me for hours.

Anger came easily. Mistakes and misunderstandings meant I was wronged. While on a trip with my mom to the Metropolitan Museum of Art in New York City, the parking attendant at the garage, which we discovered was full only after searching for a space for twenty minutes, got my wrath when she tried to charge me $25 as we were leaving. She apologized for her mistake, but my anger didn't recognize she was human. Instead, I accused her of not doing her job. If a manager had been nearby, I would have screamed that she should have been fired. *A thousand cardboard boxes*. I wasn't sure I recognized myself anymore.

The worst was when the reminder came in a place and from a person I never expected. A few weeks after everything, Kristine's family celebrated her oldest brother's engagement. She invited me to come, even though the only people I would know at this large gathering would be her and her immediate family. I went only because Kristine had invited me, my dear friend who had been there for me when I needed her most, who was one of the few people with whom I wanted to spend time anymore. Her house was familiar and safe. As I pulled up her street, I noticed cars parked along both sides. None was familiar, except for Dan's car.

I parked and approached the top of the driveway, carefully making my way down the notoriously steep hill. It was another beautiful, still day. Everyone was outside. I scanned the crowd for Dan and found him right away, talking to someone he had just met. He seemed uncomfortable to see me at first, possibly recalling the time we'd spent together in the emergency room and at my dad's funeral. Neither of us wanted to talk about it. We walked up to Kristine's brother and future sister-in-law to wish them well. She held a camera. "Do you want me to take your picture?" Dan offered.

"That would be so great!" she answered. "In fact, and I hate to ask this of you, but would you mind taking pictures with this camera all day? I don't want to be the one taking pictures. I'd rather be in them since it's our party."

She didn't know how welcomed that request was. We happily took her camera, using it as a tool to have fun and avoid conversation with others. Only when she picked up her photos after the film was developed did she see that not all of our photos were of the party. Despite the fact that Dan graduated salutatorian and eventually became a doctor, he liked making us laugh. For one of my birthdays, he gave me a large poster of Kramer from *Seinfeld*, the famous portrait, for the sole purpose of seeing me bust out in belly laughs, which was exactly what I did. Taking candid photos as well as random pictures of empty soda cans, half eaten appetizer plates, and anything else we thought was goofy made this engagement party where we hardly knew anyone an unexpected outlet of joy. So much laughter. Stomach pains from laughter. Tears-coming-from-my-eyes laughter. Laughter I didn't think would happen again.

Our laughter was interrupted when Kristine shouted a question toward me over the heads of several people. "Hey, Sue?"

"Yeah?" I turned, unprepared.

"Your dad wasn't hit by the trunk, was he?"

"No, he wasn't. He got caught up in the branches." I replied automatically without fully processing what was asked. My stomach pains from laughter immediately felt like bruises from a punch.

"I was just asking because these people knew your dad and they wanted to know," she said, gesturing to a couple I didn't recognize. *A thousand cardboard boxes.* The couple appeared horrified and awkwardly offered their condolences. Uncomfortable silence followed, all of us silently searching for the acceptable social protocol to move on. I broke it with a simple, "Excuse me," and disappeared into the crowd, grasping for the anonymity I'd had only minutes before. Then it dawned on me, Kristine was sharing this story, casually speaking about it at a crowded party, without considering my feelings.

Perhaps she had been approached by this couple who thought they recognized me from the services and wanted to know more about what happened. Perhaps it came up innocently in conversation because it was big news in town. Perhaps she wanted to show off that she was attached to the biggest story in town. Perhaps it was an entirely different scenario. But based on how she asked me, out of the blue and so carelessly, all of the scenarios I could imagine felt dirty. I felt terribly exposed and uncomfortable.

After her faux pas, Kristine didn't check on me. She didn't apologize for bringing up an extremely difficult subject. She continued mixing and mingling in the crowd, as if loudly asking me that question was not a big deal. For me, this behavior spoke volumes.

For months after that party, Kristine didn't contact me. Even though nursing school was only twenty minutes away from home, she didn't invite me to hang out. I wondered if my friend cared more about me or more about the story. The wound on our friendship never healed.

HOME WASN'T WHERE I WAS supposed to be. If I wasn't thinking about *a thousand cardboard boxes*, I thought about what I was missing. I was supposed to be making dinner for myself in my single apartment on South Campus at Syracuse University. I was supposed to be memorizing lines, auditioning for shows, stomping through the early snow on the quad, and going to parties. I was supposed to be treating myself to clothes at my favorite store, eating the best whole wheat bagel with vegetable cream cheese at the breakfast dive, and hitting the bars on Marshall Street, known to everyone local as M Street. I was supposed to be preparing for my second chance at passing my sophomore evaluation. I was supposed to be pursuing my dream of acting. But doing any of those things felt like a fight and nothing in me wanted to fight.

I didn't want to fight people who suggested I couldn't be an actress. I didn't want them to be right, but I also didn't know if I wanted that dream anymore. Imagining myself onstage, all eyes watching, didn't seem exciting anymore. Some days felt like a pressure cooker of emotions, tucked deep inside so as to not rock like I did before. Acting, at least good acting, is incredibly emotional. I didn't know if I had it in me. I needed to see if I could still do it before going back to Syracuse and potentially wasting another $50,000 of tuition money.

I found an acting studio in Manhattan that offered a Monday evening class I could afford with the pay from my clothing store job. A new routine developed of riding the train to Penn Station and walking eight blocks south on Seventh Avenue to Twenty-Sixth Street, taking the elevator to the fourth floor and walking through the small white waiting area into the black box theater—my favorite kind of stage. No one there knew anything about me—not that I'd performed in dozens of shows and filled my bookshelves with plays, not that I was a third-year acting student at Syracuse, not that I'd gone to theater camp with kids whose parents were Hollywood producers, actors, and musicians. It felt like a clean slate, like I was starting my dream over from scratch, evaluating for myself if I could still do it.

Thankfully, it was fun. Monday nights became something I looked forward to. Improvisations and voice and breathing exercises felt easy. Classes were playful. This was a beginner's class and it felt good to go back to the basics and explore what felt easy and familiar. It wasn't until ten weeks into it that it was my turn to deliver a monologue, and something felt different. I'd chosen the dramatic monologue that I'd used during my auditions for college theater programs, one that I'd worked on for years. It was a bad coincidence that the first line of the monologue was, "My father froze to death out on the street."

Before *a thousand cardboard boxes*, I thought I had reached the emotion of that character. After all, it was the monologue that got me into Syracuse. I sat in front of the class and delivered that first line and immediately felt my throat tighten, a lump rising. In this acting class where even though I had formed some friendships, I was still anonymous, and every part of me wanted to run from that emotion, to stay anonymous. My performance was flat.

Having received mostly positive feedback all along in class, the instructor sensed something was wrong. She tried to direct me, to help draw out the emotion and bring some life to my performance. Immediately I knew what she was trying to do, only realizing then how bad a choice it was for me to work on this monologue. Still, if I wanted to see if I still had it in me, I knew I had to do it, but in order to go there, I stepped out of being anonymous and told the class about my background and *a thousand cardboard boxes* and broke down in tears.

"It's too soon to do this monologue," the instructor suggested.

"I know," I replied sniffling, "but I want to see if I can still do this."

She didn't argue with me, and instead continued to give directions. After three more tries and about twenty minutes past when class was scheduled to end, I finally got to a place with the performance that was good.

"That felt much better," I said afterward.

"That was much better," she agreed as the class shared in her sentiment.

As class ended and everyone gathered their things, the instructor approached me. "You can do this," she said, "but it's not always going to be easy. You need to take care of yourself first."

I heard her loud and clear. I could do this, but did I have it in me? That was the question. After my last class before returning to Syracuse, my dream still felt uncertain.

I MADE ONE TRIP TO SYRACUSE during my semester off. It just so happened to be during the week of my twenty-first birthday, but that wasn't why I went. Every Wednesday, the entire theater department participated in a two-hour class called Theater Lab. The beginning was reserved for announcements, but the focus of the class changed every week. One week, we'd watch a faculty member directing students in a scene or a song. Another week, we'd watch junior evaluation performances. Every semester, one week's class was devoted to a panel of alumni, some of whom were acting, directing, writing, or in a completely different field. The day before my birthday, Aaron Sorkin, one of the department's most successful alumni, the man who up to that point wrote *A Few Good Men* and *An American President*, one of the most highly regarded movie and television writers in Hollywood, was scheduled to appear at Theater Lab. Of course, I had to go.

Only a small handful of friends knew I was coming. As I made my way into the theater, people greeted me with big hugs and warm wishes. Their affection tugged at me, reminding me of the camaraderie I was missing. By far, this was the most social I had been since *a thousand cardboard boxes*. Watching them interact with each other, talking about the show they were doing, struggles with classes, and gossiping about hookups and parties all accentuated how different I felt from them. Nothing in me wanted to be a junior in college. It was the last few hours before I was to turn twenty-one and I didn't want to bar hop or do any of the things most kids at Syracuse University did on that milestone birthday.

Theater Lab was a class often ditched, except for this day. Seeing over 200 students milling about the seats, it was obvious no one wanted to miss this rare opportunity. Magically, my friends and I scored house seats, right in the middle with the best view, as if I was meant to be there. His message was why I was there. A teacher we had in common, one that everyone has a class with at some point, had told me that even Aaron Sorkin had failed his sophomore evaluation. I wanted to hear him explain that, but I could only guess why everyone else came that day. I assumed it was because Aaron Sorkin is in the "big leagues," famous, and has "the in." I wanted to know why someone who had "made it" ever failed in the first place. Aside from being in the same program as he was, I imagined that was the only thing we had in common.

After being introduced, Sorkin walked out onstage, sat in a folding chair, and began to talk about his journey, which was composed of a combination of failures, including his sophomore evaluation, and passion, hard work, and good luck, like so many other success stories I'd heard before. Students asked questions, many of them focused on what his secret was, as if the answer was the key to unlocking their own paths. *How exactly did he get in? How did he connect with this or that director? How did he meet this or that producer? How did he get his foot in the door? How? How? How?*

As much as I wanted to learn the key to success, to hear an answer that would make everything happen more easily for me, it became clear to me that Aaron Sorkin's journey was unique. No one else was going to walk his path but him, and attempting to replicate his career was not going to happen.

Even though we all knew he had failed his sophomore evaluation, no one had asked about it yet. I had to know. When he stated he had time for one more question, I quickly shot my hand up, sitting upright and looking him right in the eye, hoping to grab enough of his attention that he'd have no choice but to call on me. "Yes ... you," he said, looking directly at me.

I moved forward in my seat, taking this moment to engage with him as much as possible. "You said in the beginning that you failed your sophomore evaluation. One of our instructors said that one of the main reasons students fail is because they lack confidence. Is this why you failed, and if not, why did you fail?"

He chuckled, and then said, "I think it's safe to say that confidence wasn't my problem then." He was the only one laughing, the rest of the theater stayed silent. Regardless of passing, failing, or being a freshman or sophomore and worrying about what was to come, everyone was now hanging on his words, familiar with the meaning that everyone attached to sophomore evaluations at Syracuse. "Yeah . . . ," he trailed off, clearly now the one searching for the answer. ". . . I . . . well . . . huh . . . You know, I don't know why I failed my sophomore evaluation," he finally admitted. "I have never really thought about it. I'll have to think about that one."

A friend sitting next to me leaned in and whispered in my ear, "You stumped Aaron Sorkin!"

His searching answered my question. In that moment I realized that in the grand scheme of life, with all of its triumph, tribulations, and tragedies, sophomore evaluations meant crap. Failing didn't stop Sorkin.

Sorkin's response released a weight for me. Part of me had hoped that seeing him speak would help me figure out if I still wanted to be an actress. It didn't, but it reminded me that my dream was mine and I could do whatever I wanted with it: chase it, make it, destroy it, or leave it.

Afterward, I celebrated my birthday with a small group of friends and one glass of wine, easily one of the tamest twenty-first birthday celebrations ever at Syracuse.

I KNEW IF I LEFT AROUND NOON that I'd make it home in time to go with my mom to Aunt Janice and Uncle Jeff's house in South Plainfield for my family birthday party. I got up and changed into jeans and a tee-shirt, skipping a shower, figuring I could get ready at home. I packed my car and left it parked in the lot, choosing to walk to M Street on what felt like an unusually warm morning. I only needed a light jacket.

Everywhere I glanced, I saw more reminders that life at school was continuing without me. The theater was dressed in large banners advertising *A Few Good Men*, a show I would miss. Classmates hurried to the glass entrance to the Drama Department, scanning their ID cards to unlock the door, a familiar buzz I heard all the way across the street. In the lot across from the theater, the parking attendant sat in his black folding chair next to his booth, his arms folded in front of him, looking like he had nothing to do but sit there. Walking up South Crouse Avenue, the buildings all looked the same. Traffic was no different on these streets. Turning left onto M Street, everything was still there. Most of my favorite places weren't open yet except for the bagel shop, where I got my toasted whole wheat bagel with vegetable cream cheese and an orange juice. I sat outside watching the world continue as I savored my breakfast, knowing I wouldn't have this experience again for months.

I had time to walk up University Avenue, one of my favorite routes toward campus. Its hill leads right up to Hall of Languages, the iconic building of the entire university. Its Onondaga limestone, second empire architecture reeks of academia with east and west cupolas balancing a large clock tower. I hoped one of my classes would be taught within its walls, even though rumor had it that students who were lucky to have classes there were disappointed by its interior. The grandness of the building always took my breath away. Just looking at it made me feel smarter.

I had forgotten about the Pan Am Flight 103 memorial that sat in front of the building. As I approached, I noticed its curved wall, which included an inscription:

This place of remembrance is dedicated to the memory of the 35 students enrolled in Syracuse University's Division of International Programs Abroad who died with 235 others as the result of a plane crash December 21, 1988 over Lockerbie Scotland caused by a terrorist bomb.

Every other time I'd passed the memorial I hadn't bothered to stop. Now, it was hard to walk away. I remembered watching the news and seeing the nose of the plane crumpled on the green grass, not understanding what terrorism was or why someone would want to do that to an airplane filled with people. Now, it was a reminder that everything could change in a second.

DRIVING HOME, I THOUGHT about my question to Aaron Sorkin, amazed that he didn't have anything close to an answer. He was no different from me, fumbling through challenges like the rest of us, but still finding success and happiness. Unknowingly, he had made me feel like I'd be okay. I continued to think about what he shared about his career, so much so that I didn't realize I was on Route 80 West closing in on Hazelton, Pennsylvania, the complete opposite direction of home.

I slowed down, pulled over to the shoulder, and looked around. *Did I really pass a sign that said Hazelton was the next exit?* Cars whipped by as I sat looking around, hoping the changing color of the trees looked familiar. It didn't look much different than where I was supposed to be, but it didn't feel right. I carefully pulled back onto the road, realizing I couldn't determine where I was exactly until I saw the next sign. Sure enough, the next exit was for Hazelton.

Fuck. Shit. Damn it. Shit. Shit . . . was all that my mind could think about as I realized my mistake. Since these were the days before cell phones and GPS were common, I took the exit, hoping to find a store or a fast food restaurant that would have a pay phone, only to be welcomed by more unfamiliar trees. Rather than waste more time, I searched for the ramp for Route 80 East, speeding toward it once I saw the sign.

I had already cut it close by leaving Syracuse with only just enough time to get home, shower, and change in time for my birthday party with my family. This directional mistake added an unknown amount of time to my drive, only to also include highway construction in Scranton, an accident on the S curves on the New Jersey side of the Delaware Water Gap, and the beginnings of rush hour by the time I got home. I ran inside, noticing my mom had already left, assuming she'd meet me at Aunt Janice and Uncle Jeff's house. Looking at the time, I was supposed to be at their house already. I called them, explaining I was on my way. I knew that a lot of people were waiting for me.

I didn't have time to shower. I was still wearing my tee-shirt and jeans. Glancing in the mirror before running out the door, I accepted that I was at the very least presentable.

More rush hour traffic thickened along the route that usually takes an hour when no one is on the road. I arrived two hours late, and I hate being late.

Greeted by a living room with presents, appetizers, wine and concerned faces, I explained what happened. "I wasn't paying attention and I went on 80 West instead of 80 East and didn't realize it until I was all the way to the Hazelton exit. I can't believe I did that! I hate that I'm late!"

What followed was a chorus of "I've-done-that-before."

"I've done that before and ended up in Pennsylvania."

"I've done that before on the Parkway, going north when I wanted to go south."

"I've done that on the Parkway too, twice coming out of a rest stop and not paying attention."

"The worst is doing that on the Turnpike. Then there's no chance of turning around without it taking an extra hour at least."

"I've done that before and nearly ended up in the Holland Tunnel, which would have been hell."

"Have you ever mistaken 278 for 287. It's not pretty."

"There's a 278? Where the heck does that take you?"

"Staten Island."

"Oh my."

Light conversation. Everyone politely sitting around, avoiding any reference to the one person missing. A changed dynamic being felt out for the first time while I opened gifts. I opened several "twenty-first birthday" cards, celebrating that I no longer needed fake IDs and could go crazy drinking anything I wanted, a rite of passage that seemed trivial. The last card took me aback, its soft colors and script signifying the opposite sentiment of all the others. I opened it and before I could finish reading the inside, I scanned down to see who the card was from. I should have seen it coming, but I wasn't prepared to see "Mom" . . . one name all by itself.

ACTING CLASS IN MANHATTAN ended late. Rather than taking the train home, every Monday night I'd hop on the subway to the Upper West Side to stay at Uncle Bill and Susan's apartment. Every visit, Uncle Bill and I talked late into the night. Often the conversation led back to my dad.

"I'll never forget the last thing I said to your dad," Uncle Bill began.

I was intrigued immediately, remembering my last words to him. *I love you and I'll see you later.* If there had to be final words, I was happy with them.

"It was about two weeks before when the three of us were at Yankee Stadium for the game."

I had forgotten that we had gone to the game. It instantly hit me how fitting it was that Yankee Stadium was the last place my dad and Uncle Bill saw each other. Both grew up being huge fans, collecting a ton of baseball cards, all of them thrown out by my grandmother before anyone realized their value. They'd been to the stadium so many times, seen so many historic baseball moments over the course of nearly five decades.

"You were there when I said it," he said.

"I was?"

"You don't remember?"

The wheels turned in my head, attempting to put myself back there. "I remember saying good-bye to you outside of the stadium as we were walking toward the parking lot and you had to go to the subway." My mind drew a blank.

"But you don't remember what I said."

I had no idea. I imagined it was something perfect, thoughtful, just the right way to unknowingly end the five decades of brotherhood these two had built. Something to cherish and hold on to forever.

"I really can't think," I admitted. "I remember it was crowded, so maybe I didn't hear you."

Uncle Bill had a look on his face, an expression with a smile and a regret at the same time.

"Come on! What did you say??"

"I told him I had to hit the john to go piss."

I couldn't help laughing, and Uncle Bill laughed with me.

Call it too much bad luck. Uncle Bill had had a lot of experience with death. His dad died at fifty-two from Hodgkin's lymphoma. His baby son died from a number of health complications. His wife died at forty-six when she did not wake up from cardiac-related surgery. Now his brother was gone. Despite all this loss, Uncle Bill still walked around generally happy.

I still couldn't imagine ever feeling happy. It dawned on me that maybe I could learn from Uncle Bill. "You know, Uncle Bill, you're a happy guy considering everything that's happened to you."

He thought about this for a moment. "You know, you're right. I mean, I'm not all that happy *now*."

"Well, obviously not *now*."

"But I get what you're saying."

"Really though. You've lost your dad, your son, your wife, and now your brother. Even when I was a kid, you had lost your dad and son only a year before I was born, but you always came across to me as the happy, fun uncle wanting to play and get into a little trouble."

"You know, it's interesting that you say that because just the other day one of my friends said the same thing to me."

Clearly, I wasn't the only one that noticed.

Uncle Bill went on. "He asked me how I can even move on in life and get out of bed with everything I've been through. He said to me, 'Bill, how do you do this? How do you go through all of this? You've lost your dad, your son, your wife and now your brother. I mean, that's *a lot*. That's *a lot* of shit.' And I just told him. 'Yeah, that is a lot of shit, but everyone's got shit.'" He got up from his chair. "You wanna Fudgsicle? I'm gonna get a Fudgsicle."

"Sure."

"These are good and Susan allows me to have them," he reasoned as he walked down the hall towards the kitchen.

He'd hit me with that one piece of wisdom said in the only way Uncle Bill could say it, punctuated by a Fudgsicle. It stuck with me. It revealed to me that I was no different from anyone else.

CHAPTER 3

Forward and Backward

A WEEK AFTER RETURNING to Syracuse several months later, I found myself running into the bathroom outside of the Drama Department's administrative offices, breaking down after an instructor that I tremendously admired simply told me no. Because I had taken the previous semester off, I didn't have the advantage of registering for classes early and this instructor's scene study class was full with a long waiting list, for good reason. Geri Clark was the best. Of the dozens of faculty members in the entire department, a very small number of teachers knew how to build a student's abilities from a positive approach like Geri. She was one of those instructors who knew how to highlight a student's strengths and provide thought-provoking directions that often led to a beautiful shift in that student's performance, like watching a plant bloom right before your eyes. Witnessing this growth was one of the reasons why I loved acting.

Unfortunately, not every instructor at Syracuse had this approach. Some were very negative, even resorting to mind games, like saying to a student in front of a large class, "I would *never* cast *you*." It was a tone that these particular instructors said was pervasive within the entertainment industry. They validated their methods by explaining that students needed to be prepared to perform at their best within that type of environment. Even though I had been able to get into a different class with a different instructor, it was one I didn't know who my friends told me was in the category of the negative instructors. I believed if I didn't get into Geri's class I would be setting myself up for failure.

I knew it was a tall order to ask Geri to make an exception and allow me into her class. I knew a no was probably coming, but my reaction hit me like the time the rusty nail punctured my foot at the beach in Wildwood. The bubble that contained my emotions popped again; and just as Geri turned to walk away from me the flood gates opened and I felt myself about to drop in the middle of the hallway. Thankfully, the bathroom was right next to me and I was able to duck into it with only one friend, Jennifer, witnessing the ordeal. It just so happened that Jennifer was dating the son of one of my dad's golf friends. Having seen me at the wake and knowing the truth of *a thousand cardboard boxes*, she understood why I was crying without needing to ask. She took control of the situation, asking people to use a different bathroom to give me privacy while she calmed me down. Afterward, she drove me home to my apartment.

I went to my bedroom and nestled into the black leather bean bag chair at the foot of my bed, my go-to comfort spot. Even though I was only in my new apartment for a week, this bean bag chair quickly became the place where I'd collapse after unpacking or a long day of classes. I collapsed often. The cool leather quickly warmed up once I settled in, enveloping me in a way that felt safe, subduing any effects of stress from moving forward from *a thousand cardboard boxes.*

My next class wasn't for several hours and it was up the hill. I killed my time watching the *Game Show Network* and wondering, *What next?* I visualized myself going to the scene study class I was enrolled in and being told I was terrible or that I had no business being there. My bubble would burst again, in front of the entire class. I wanted to avoid that happening at all costs.

I wondered, *If I could ignore the feedback, would I still have any magical moments of growth?*

The more I thought about going to class, the more I remembered the many negative comments I had heard from instructors over the previous two years, the more I thought about the emotional work acting requires, and the more I felt myself detaching from my dream. And then the big thought hit me—*could I get up on stage in front of an audience and allow myself to be judged?*

Emotion is a major requirement for acting. I thought about emotions. Five years before at theater camp, I had the privilege of being cast in *Playing for Time,* a play adapted from the film written by Arthur

Miller and Fania Fénelon about Fénelon's experience as a female prisoner in Auschwitz. I played one of the prisoners. Before doing the production, I knew nothing about the Holocaust. After watching several documentaries and doing a reenactment exercise carefully created by the director to help us better understand what being captured by the Nazis may have been like, my feelings toward acting grew much more profound. It was my favorite production of all time, even though it required crying, screaming, and being beaten in the final scene. It taught me that theater, television, and film can be incredible vehicles for enlightening others, for making an impact on the world. Even though I had wanted to be a professional actress before this play, the experience lit a flame in me, giving me a reason to act.

Then there was *Antigone* and *Twelfth Night*, both of which I did in high school. In the beginning, I had no idea what I was saying and I'm pretty sure the rest of the cast had no idea what they were saying either. My initial goal was to remember my lines; and again, I bet I wasn't the only one with that goal. In time and with a lot of direction, we found the emotion and brought Greek tragedy and Shakespeare to life. Suddenly, the rhythm of the lines clicked, like learning a new instrument. I thought about how empowered I felt after those productions.

My last play, *No Exit*, was about nine months before *a thousand cardboard boxes*. It was a student production directed by my good friend Vik, who admitted to me after the show that the only reason he cast me was because I was the only one who came in with the longest monologue memorized during the first audition. I wasn't the best actress up for the part, but he believed in me and my work ethic. It was a difficult show to perform because there was no intermission and I was onstage continuously from nearly the beginning to the end, which was about ninety minutes of staying in character in a black box theater with nowhere to hide or take any sort of break. I learned a lot about my stamina from that production.

I thought about all of those shows and the fun musicals, the silly plays, the scenes in class that were difficult, and the scenes that seemed like a waste of time. All seemed so far away. The thought of doing *Playing for Time* again, once my favorite production, now turned my stomach. The idea of purposely re-calling an emotion for the sake of a show scared me. Worst of all, the thought of being judged for a perfor-mance that I had put everything into, emotions and all, made me cringe. The more I thought about it, im-agining what may be ahead, even with fond memo-ries, the more I began to accept that perhaps *a thou-sand cardboard boxes* was taking something else away from me that I loved. I said it in my head for the first time, *I don't want to be an actress anymore.*

It didn't feel like a loss. If anything, it felt like a re-lease. Immediately, it felt easier to breathe.

I stayed curled up in the black leather bean bag chair and felt the release. My chest no longer felt tight. My shoulders relaxed. I clicked the remote and turned off the television. I looked toward the win-dows and noticed the sun shining on the tree branches. It was fall, but it might as well have been winter since the leaves were long gone. The bright blue sky appeared warmer than it was. Soon I would need to put on my boots and winter coat and make my way up the hill for my next class, *Women in Art.* It was only the third class, but it was already one of my favorites. The professor lectured beautifully, showing slides of paintings and explaining the history of women during the time period and why they were depicted in the manner seen in the piece. Clearly, this was her passion course, the class that was the reason she taught. She had written the textbook. I looked forward to spending ninety minutes sitting at a desk in the dark taking notes as the professor spoke eloquently from memory without stopping.

As I continued to stare out the windows, think about my next class, and contemplate more classes like that up the hill, the phone shattered the silence. I jumped in my bean bag chair, startled from the ringing. My heart began to race. I picked up the phone. It was Geri Clark. She excitedly told me that she changed her mind and would be delighted to have me in her class.

"Oh wow, Geri," I struggled for words. "You didn't have to do that. I know you have a lot of people wanting to join your class."

"It's okay!" she reassured. "I'm letting everyone on the wait list into my class. It'll be big, but we'll get it done and it'll be alright."

It felt like a second chance I didn't need. I thanked her profusely, and feeling like I couldn't say no, I told her I'd be at her next class where I'd give it my all.

"I know you will! I'm so happy you'll be in my class! You have a good day and I'll see you Thursday. Bye-bye!" She hung up.

I don't know what changed her mind. I wondered if Jennifer had said something. But I did know that my mind was made up about changing my career path.

I DID NOT TELL ANYONE about my decision. I'd gone this far, I still wanted a college degree and I had only three semesters remaining in order to graduate on time, but my semester was set, and I had to take the scene study class as well as my other acting classes and my classes up the hill. At this point, I didn't need to change anything. Either my senior year would be only acting classes, or it would be a minor concentration of my choosing. Technically, I didn't even need to decide that until the end of the semester, but because I already had Fine Arts credits and since all my classes up the hill were Fine Arts classes, I knew that would be my minor concentration. I accepted the journey of the "fallback plan," which I proudly stopped imagining as such. Now I envisioned a Bachelor of Science degree framed and hanging on my wall.

Passing my sophomore evaluation was no longer necessary, but I wanted to pass it anyway, simply for the satisfaction of truly knowing that I could do it. Knowing that the stakes were no longer high, scene study class became fun. I was more interested in rooting for my classmates and watching them grow, knowing that dream of a professional life as an actor was very much alive for each of them. When it came time for me to perform my scene, which fortunately was a fun, comedic scene, I took risks, not caring about the outcome of what the students and instructor thought. It paid off in the feedback. I did some of my best work in that class. Acting became something I loved again, even though I didn't want to pursue it as a career.

And even while I rehearsed my sophomore evaluation scene with my friend Heather, who was facing her last chance at passing.

And even while walking out in front of the entire faculty to perform our scene . . . even while noticing one faculty member sitting back in his chair, arms crossed in front of him with a "I could give a fuck" look on his face, one of the negative instructors who was particularly hard on me the year before.

And even after Geri proudly told me I passed my sophomore evaluation.

I HAD TO FIND a new dream, a new purpose. *A thousand cardboard boxes* changed me. I felt so far away from that person, the one who grew up without any significant scars. I didn't know where I was going, but after hearing about a college summer internship program at Walt Disney World while out to dinner with family friends, I knew I was going there. They loved everything Disney. Their son had completed the program and found that it opened doors to different job opportunities, not to mention that it was a great conversation starter in his interviews. They could not say enough about the program, and it was all we could talk about during the entire dinner. To get paid while working in the parks and attending business classes at the "happiest place on earth" appeared like a golden path, the one where I would triumph over grief and fear and find a new direction. My application was submitted and accepted.

Two days after the spring semester ended, I drove down to Orlando, Florida, in my white Chevy Cavalier convertible, feeling a sense of freedom with each passing state. I sped for most of the way, the white road lines flashing by, counting down my miles to discovery, to a quest for happiness in all aspects of my life. The sun shone the entire way down, each changing landscape's vibrancy pulsing with beauty, as if every possible sign from the universe screamed to me *YES!*

Yes, to something new. Yes, to change. Yes, to happiness.

I knew little as to what to expect. I knew I'd be living in a three-bedroom, two-bath apartment on Disney property with five other girls. I knew I'd work in a restaurant at one of the parks. I knew I'd have business classes one day per week. I knew I'd earn minimum wage. From that, I hoped to find my purpose, have some adventures, and gain a new happiness that for too many months I thought I'd never find.

I knew I had unique reasons for participating in the program, but it was completely naive of me to assume that most of the other thousand or so participants had the same ambitious agenda as me. This dawned on me as I first walked into the apartment and I was greeted by heaps of stuff. Moving boxes, luggage, and shopping bags sat in cluttered piles with giggly girls and nervous parents milling around them like a swarm of happy bees, all attempting to arrange a honeycomb in a hive. My two black suitcases were my first indication that I wouldn't fit into the mold. The swarm was so busy chatting, sorting, and unpacking they didn't notice me standing in the doorway, wondering how I would enter without getting stung.

Without smoke or a protective suit, I treaded cautiously. "*Uh* . . . hi everyone."

The swarm stopped what they were doing and moved toward me. "Hi!"

"Oh, you must be our last suitemate!"

"It's so nice to meet you!"

"Where's the rest of your stuff?"

"Where are your parents?"

"Where are you from?"

"Your mom and dad let you drive down here all by yourself?"

"Oh my god! We're at Disney!"

"We're going to have so much fun this summer!"

"We're going to be best friends!"

"We're going to be bridesmaids at each other's weddings!"

"It'll be the six of us forever!"

I offered timid one-word answers as questions flew, overwhelmed by their enthusiasm, which ought to have been a welcomed embrace. While driving down to Florida for two days, I thought about nothing but my future, knowing that I didn't have answers as to what that would evolve to become but trusting the process ahead. Oddly, I'd arrived at Disney not even thinking about fun, and here I was greeted by five bright, vibrant girls who exuded fun. That's not to say that I didn't picture myself riding Space Mountain whenever I wanted, but my focus was laser sharp on finding my purpose. Having let go of my desire to pursue acting and being twenty-one years old with only one year of college left gave me anxiety about the inevitable…*What happens next?* Now that *a thousand cardboard boxes* had opened my eyes to the fact that life can change in an instant, control over situations became comforting.

"You're the last one here, so this is your bed!"

The decisions of which hexagon in the honeycomb was already made for me . . . mine would be the bed closest to the door to the hallway, farthest from any window. It seemed the least desirable. It wasn't a space that exuded peace. It looked like the bed reserved for someone who didn't care much about sleep, for a worker bee whose needs no one considered. It was a bed that others felt served its purpose. Superficially, why would anyone complain about it?

It would have been nice to pick beds as a group, but given my roommates' excitement, it was clear that no one else thought the decision mattered—and it probably didn't much. I wished it wasn't a big deal for me, that I could easily slip in and go with the flow, but for reasons that are unclear to me even to this day, it felt like a big deal. Nonetheless, I kept my resentment to myself.

"I thought I'd take this dresser and this part of the closet and then you can have all of this," my roommate offered.

Another hexagon, this time a generous one, with more than enough hanging space and another dresser.

"Thank you," I replied appreciatively. The bed now felt less like a big deal. Still, while observing my roommates unpack, already sharing clothing and jewelry, their faces beaming with an innocent excitement as they hugged their parents goodbye, even before learning anything about them I decided they were different from me. I wished I could be like them, because on the surface they seemed untainted, like they'd never been through anything hard or sad like me.

Later that day, as we all sat together in the living room talking, I learned otherwise. One roommate grew up without her father. Her mother had eventually remarried, and she embraced her stepfather as her own. Her face held a constant smile, as if her life was breezy, even though she recalled times when her family struggled to put food on the table. I wished I was like her, even though her life did not sound easy, yet somehow, she managed to be carefree now, seemingly unaffected by her past. Her smile made her story seem unreal, even though it was the truth.

Another roommate from Minnesota, who happened to be the spitting image of Alice from *Alice in Wonderland* with her perfect blond hair, bright blue eyes, and radiant smile, had watched her house burn to the ground a few years before because it was winter, and all the fire hydrants were frozen. Initially it was discovered as a small fire in the garage, but by the time everyone had escaped it was too large to fight without the help from firefighters. Her mom managed to grab a few photos, but otherwise her family lost everything. She spoke about things that could not be replaced. She was thankful that no one was harmed.

As she spoke, I could tell that this event still bothered her, but up to that point, her positive attitude made it easy to assume she'd never been through anything traumatic.

Realizing that these girls might not be as different from me as I thought, I shared *a thousand cardboard boxes*. I explained the previous ten months had been a hard time for me and that the anniversary of the day of the storm would be coming up in two months and I felt anxious about that date. None of the other girls had lost a parent, so I didn't expect them to understand. But their hugs afterward gave me hope that they would be there for me when the time came.

"Let's go have some fun," the girl with the breezy attitude suggested, a welcomed change from sitting in the living room talking about our traumas.

"Let's go to the parks!" another exclaimed.

We piled into my car and my other roommate's car and drove to the Magic Kingdom. It was late in the day, and by the time we parked and made our way to the entrance, we only had time for one ride. We headed for Thunder Mountain. We got to ride it twice in a row, the last two times it would operate for the day. During the final ride, fireworks lit up the dimming summer sky that moments before was a classic Florida pink sunset. Smiling, laughing, screaming with excitement, it felt like an awesome beginning. Everything felt righter than it had since *a thousand cardboard boxes.*

I WENT GROCERY SHOPPING alone without my roommates, something I did often to escape from them. It was easier to go alone. The first time was a mess. The morning after our amazing night at Magic Kingdom, we piled into my car and my roommate's car and went on our first grocery shopping trip. It wasn't until we had arrived and shopped for a twenty minutes that it was revealed to me that none of my roommates had ever shopped for groceries, and looking at the five bottles of ketchup, five jars of mustard, ten boxes of pasta, ten jars of tomato sauce, five gallons of milk, five gallons of orange juice and countless boxes of frozen dinners, I suggested we share some things. I was outvoted, even after I reminded them of the size of our refrigerator. Driving back to our apartment with grocery bags jammed into both trunks and in every free corner of space inside both cars, my roommates laughed at the adventure while I cringed. I felt different again.

A few days later, while at an outdoor mall, we happened upon a sale at Victoria's Secret. The sales associate at the register suggested we each open a credit card to receive an extra discount. She processed each application, and a few were either declined or needed further processing. Mine was processed and immediately I was issued a credit card with a $1,000 limit, which the sales associate noted out loud, "Wow, that's one of the highest limits I've ever seen!" As we left the store, one of my roommates asked me how my application got processed so fast and with such a high limit. From that conversation, I learned that not everyone in our group had a credit card of her own. I also learned that everyone either lived on campus or lived at home and commuted to school. A few didn't know how to write a check. One came with me to the bank so she could learn how to cash her paycheck. For some, this was their first job, and learning how to juggle staying out late and making it to work on time had a learning curve. Rather than viewing their innocence to the world as their starting point and recognizing that everyone begins somewhere, I saw my roommates as naive and sheltered, and so far away from me. Each question they asked me was a reminder of *a thousand cardboard boxes*, of why I was different.

I didn't want the reminder. This time shopping alone, I had a very long list of requests from my roommates, and subsequently, an overflowing shopping cart, including three gallons of milk, four gallons of orange juice, four boxes of pasta, four jars of sauce, and a countless number of frozen pizzas and cereal boxes mixed in with the carrots, humus, eggs, and bread that were the reason for me needing to go to the store in the first place.

Just as I walked out toward the parking lot with my heavy cart, the sky opened up. In the summertime, Florida tends to have a daily afternoon rain shower. It usually passes quickly and helps cool things off for a moment. While at work, a frequent question we would get from Disney guests is when the rain is supposed to stop. As much as we tried to provide the best service and give the most amazing experience to the guests, this was, for common sense reasons, an impossible question to answer. Disney guests had been made to feel like anything was possible, so why wouldn't we know what Mother Nature intended for a rain shower that was preventing their family from walking to the next ride?

I was at work the first time that a storm came while I was in Florida. Standing at my hostess stand greeting guests, the rain fell heavily. Guests scrambled to find cover, many crowding together under the awning in front of the restaurant. My eyes were captivated. It was coming down hard and soaking. As the wind picked up, I jumped at the sound of a clap of thunder in the distance. My heart started to pound. *Rain. Wind. Thunder . . . a thousand cardboard boxes.*

Anxiety crept in. *Flashing emergency lights. The stretcher. The tree . . . a thousand cardboard boxes.*

The inevitable question interrupted my flashbacks. "When will it stop raining?" a worried mother with her son by her side asked me.

I turned to her, noticing her deep distress, concern written all over her face at the thought of this storm interrupting the well-planned itinerary she had probably spent months thinking about in order to make sure her family saw as much of Disney as possible. "I wish I could tell you, but storms can be quick, or they can take a while," I explained. *The responders. My friend Kim looking me in the eye while carrying a first aid kit.*

Even more distressed, she asked, "So you don't know when it'll stop?"

I was warned that guests could be relentless with weather questions. I wanted her to go away and wait patiently. "I don't know. Hopefully soon." *Wind. Sideways. Mail strewn about.*

"Is there someone else who may be able to tell us when it's going to stop raining?"

My legs felt weak. *Head turned to the side, eyes open, vacant stare.* I wanted to smack her. A coworker who had over ten years of experience overheard everything and stepped in. "It'll stop eventually. The animation tour is just around the corner if you want to do that. It's about twenty minutes long and it's all indoors. There's a chance that by the time you're done with that the rain will have stopped."

"Oh perfect! Thank you!" I watched as she grabbed her son's hand and darted over to her husband and daughter, and then the four of them running toward the entrance to the tour.

"Gotta love those questions," my coworker joked with me.

"Thanks," I replied. *The tree, a thousand cardboard boxes . . .* "I'll be right back." Wanting to fold myself into a cocoon momentarily until the storm passed, I headed toward the bathroom and chose a stall as my protective shell.

These afternoon rain showers and thunderstorms were the first ones I experienced after *a thousand cardboard boxes*. Thunderstorms aren't common in the fall in New Jersey and I don't recall ever previously experiencing any as severe as the ones in Florida. Winter in New Jersey came only with snow. Syracuse, New York, in the spring is really an extended winter. In Florida, there was a storm nearly every day. A light rain shower was nice. Seeing the steam rise from the hot pavement, cooling the summer air, was refreshing.

But often, there were thunderstorms. They came with rain, wind, thunder, and lightning . . . along with palpitations, nervousness, shortness of breath, and anxiety. Thunder made me jump out of my skin. It was like watching everything happen again and again. Every time the wind gusted, I'd think of the tree breaking apart. *A thousand cardboard boxes.* I did what I could to avoid them, usually finding an area inside a building away from windows. That time, it was the bathroom at work. I didn't want to see it, hear it, smell it, or feel it.

The storm that came up as I was exiting the grocery store was the strongest I had seen yet. Rain streamed down heavily as I stood under the covered area outside the doors. I noticed people walking out to their cars despite knowing that they would get completely drenched. I wondered how they were able to walk in the rain like it was no big deal. Too nervous to do the same, I chose to wait it out, hoping the rain would end soon. But the rain didn't end. It got heavier. The winds picked up and one of the loudest bolts of lightning I'd ever heard struck nearby.

I jumped, feeling the electricity buzzing lightly on my skin. That lightning bolt was close enough that it made people finally stop in their tracks and wait alongside me. The covered area was getting crowded with people and shopping carts. Some squeezed past us and made their way to their cars apparently without worrying about flying debris hitting them.

It was very warm out. I looked down at my cart . . . my very full, perishable cart. I wondered how long this storm was going to last before I needed to worry about everything spoiling. The fact that we were halfway through the summer and my roommates still hadn't learned that all of these groceries wouldn't fit into our refrigerator irritated me. Rather than tell them I wouldn't go shopping for them, I chose to keep the peace, since I was one of the only ones with a car and no good excuse for saying no. I knew they wouldn't understand why all of their groceries were spoiled, so without hesitation I turned to the woman next to me who also had a full shopping cart and I asked her that impossible question, "How long do you think this will last?"

She looked at me, then down at my cart, then back at me. "There's a storm every day. Could be another minute. Could be an hour. You never know."

I weighed my options. I could wait, hoping that the storm would end soon, and the groceries won't spoil, or I could make a dash for my car, hoping that I could load over a dozen bags quickly. For me, there was only one option. I waited.

"I guess I'm going to get wet," the woman said to me. "I can't wait all day. I have kids to pick up and dinner to make." I watched her walk out to her car and load everything up while the rain, wind, and lightning crashed around her. For the next ten minutes, I watched others come out of the grocery store, stop and notice the torrential rain, and walk to their cars, continuing on with their lives while I stood stuck in place—stuck in fear, stuck in anxiety, and stuck in *a thousand cardboard boxes.*

I went back inside, hoping the air conditioning would help prevent the food from spoiling. A store employee noticed me walking back in with a full cart of bagged groceries. "Is everything okay?" he asked.

"Yes, thank you. I'm just waiting out the storm and I figured the air conditioning will help keep my groceries."

The employee looked at me confused. "Is it really that bad out? I thought it was just a little rain."

"There was a lot of lightning," I explained, hoping that would be enough for him to understand.

"Oh, okay." He still looked confused. "I see you have a lot of milk. You know it can't last all that long . . ."

"I know," I snapped back. "I just can't go out in that storm."

He looked taken aback. "Okay. Well . . . just know you may lose your milk."

I had been waiting for over twenty minutes. There was no way to know when the storm would stop. It could end in seconds. It could go on for hours. I didn't want the food to spoil and I wasn't sure how much longer I could wait. I went back outside. It was still raining hard, but the wind wasn't as strong.

Make a run for it. Everyone else is. You can do this. You'll be fine.

I can't.

Yes, you can. Waiting here isn't normal. No one else is. Just go out to the car. It'll be okay.

I really don't want to.

Just do it! You're fine! You're functioning well! Don't be a crazy person!

I don't want to be crazy. I don't want to be different. I want to be normal and do what everyone else can do. I took a deep breath, aimed my cart toward my car, got ready, and ran. I ran, pushing a heavy cart, all the way to my car. The rain started to get heavier just as I popped open the trunk and quickly threw in the bags. I had only been out in the rain for about fifteen seconds and already I was soaked. I loaded up my car as fast as I could. I moved the cart out of the way, unlocked my door, and hopped in.

BANG . . . Bang bang . . . bang . . . Another lightning strike nearby. It was followed by a gust of wind that was strong enough to shake my car. I started the car and threw the gearshift into drive. I began to shake, on the verge of being overcome by fear and anxiety, and fought tears as I drove back to the apartment, thinking about *a thousand cardboard boxes.*

I didn't tell my suitemates that their milk might be spoiled. One noted that it "tasted different," but no one got sick and no one complained. I didn't want to explain, but I didn't give them a chance to understand.

AS THE SUMMER PROGRESSED, I watched them party, stay out late, go to work hung over, and seemingly not care about the opportunity that came with being a part of the college internship program. I made sure I was at work early and sometimes I'd stay late if the opportunity was there to make extra money and build relationships. My tenacity earned me a meeting with my manager, who subsequently initiated a day for me of shadowing a stage manager for *Beauty and the Beast,* which performed several times per day. I spent the day sitting in the booth listening to her call cues and manage a large cast and crew. Between shows she asked me what I wanted to do and what my goals were. I shared that I was an acting major at Syracuse University, but that I was looking for something else although I wasn't sure what. She told me about her own journey in the theater, which opened my mind even more to what I had available to me. With Disney being an entertainment company, now was the time to explore the opportunities.

My quest for a purpose began to take shape. After that day of shadowing, I was more committed to being at work, participating in the business classes, and learning as much about the Disney Company as possible. I asked questions all the time. I took extra shifts whenever possible. I worked on my portfolio, an assignment from the business classes that was not required, but would earn the participant a "Ducktorate" certificate upon completion. I went above and beyond the assignment, including write-ups about my shadowing experience and other aspects of Disney that I felt were important. Not only did I earn a Ducktorate, I also earned a "Pass the Torch" recognition, which is only awarded to one or two participants in the entire college program each trimester.

Getting out of bed early in the morning became easy. Work was fun. I barely saw my roommates. Nearly every night they'd ask me to go out with them. I said no each time instead. I spent time with other college program participants who were driven, who had also lived on their own, gone grocery shopping, and knew how to manage credit cards and bills.

Four mornings per week, my alarm woke me at 5:00 am for an early shift. I'd quietly get up, shower, and be out the door by 5:45 am. Everyone else in the apartment stayed sleeping. I was always the first one to go to bed, knowing that I felt better with at least nine hours of sleep every night. Each morning I'd wake up to a mess in the kitchen and whatever remnants of drinking or snacking or fooling around in the living room remained. Each time it reminded me that I was on a path to success. Less than a year ago, I didn't want to get out of bed.

It didn't occur to me to question whether I was missing out on any fun.

TIME TICKED ONWARD. Work shifts and classes built on themselves. With each rising and setting sun I grew more excited about what could be ahead. I envisioned living in a small one-bedroom apartment, driving to and from work, and being on my own, independent and happy. Every day felt like a step in the right direction.

Until August. Time seemed to count down. August 13th . . . August 14th . . . August 15th . . . time marched towards the one-year anniversary of my dad's death.

Despite my visions and the effort I put into creating a new purpose and the happiness it brought me, I could not stop my mind from thinking about the events from the year before. August 16th . . . *the still summer morning, my dad coming home from playing golf, wanting to go out shopping with me. Butterfly Kisses.* I cut short that thought and decided to get out.

Before *a thousand cardboard boxes*, I had loved adventure. I decided to go to Epcot Center and walk around the World Showcase. I started in Mexico and wandered into the Mayan Pyramid. I loved the inside, which appeared as a gorgeous night in a small Mexican town. Next I walked the cobblestone courtyard in Norway and watched tourists taking their pictures with trolls while wearing Viking horns. I passed through the gate toward the Temple of Heaven in China and arrived just in time to watch the acrobat troop of children perform their amazing moves. Next was Germany, where I stopped for a hot, fresh soft pretzel. I sat on a bench that overlooked the large lagoon that revealed a fantastic view of the iconic Spaceship Earth. As I sat there, I heard someone bellowing out a beautiful aria.

After I finished my pretzel, I stepped over to Italy and saw a small crowd gathered around a large man, the source of the aria. Not dressed in any special uniform and without a name tag, it was unclear if he was a Disney employee or a guest caught up in the moment. Either way, he captivated a number of people and earned a large applause when the song ended. The crowd then dispersed, and I walked over to America. I didn't stop, figuring I was already here.

I meandered around Japan admiring rows of stacked dishes and around Morocco feeling the soft texture of rugs. I grabbed a croissant in France before crossing the bridge into the United Kingdom to look at finely knit wool sweaters and Celtic jewelry. My last stop was Canada, where I viewed the film *O Canada* in the 360-degree movie theater, one of my favorite attractions in all of Epcot. That is how I spent the anniversary of *a thousand cardboard boxes,* and luckily that sound did not come to mind.

August 17th was the day of the surgery. I got up with the intention of spending the day at Magic Kingdom. It was more crowded than usual, enough so to make it unenjoyable, so I left and headed for Celebration, a real, inhabitable town Disney had only recently developed. It was so new, in fact, that the trees and landscaping were far from maturity. New roads and houses continued to be built. The downtown was small and sparse. I imagined myself living there and being a part of its growth. It seemed like the most perfect place to start a life. I parked my white convertible in front of the bank and went inside to cash my paycheck. Then I walked around the nearby neighborhood of small- to medium-sized homes. Each one was nicer than the next. Fresh paint. Charming architecture. But as beautiful as Celebration was, it looked desolate. Hardly anyone was outside. The swings at the playground drifted with the breeze. My car sat by itself among the rows of parking spaces in the center of town. A lonely fresh start. I hoped it would survive so that I could one day live there.

The summer heat intensified. I made my way back to my car and headed for Downtown Disney. After browsing the many stores, I met up with family friends for dinner, the ones who had told me about the college program in the first place. This week was their annual trip to Disney. We talked about their vacation and my experiences in the college program and earning the "Pass the Torch" award, which would look good on my resume. They acknowledged that recognition was a big deal and could open doors immediately for me at Disney. Although they had been at the funeral and knew what happened, it was never mentioned during our visit. I didn't know if they had forgotten it was the anniversary of my dad's passing or if they purposely kept themselves from bringing it up. Either way, I didn't think about it when I was with them and perhaps I came close to forgetting it.

While driving back to the apartment after dinner, I realized I hadn't shed a tear all day. I didn't shake. I didn't rock. I had a good day.

I arrived at my apartment and discovered my roommates were throwing a party with the guys from across the hall. It was already a loud, irritating mess. Beer bottles and boxes on the kitchen counter, alcohol banners hung everywhere, the door wide open with no one inside. Everyone was over at the guys' apartment. Although I'd told them about the anniversary date I was struggling with at the beginning of the summer, I'd never reminded them that it was this day. Still the timing proved their insensitivity to my needs. I walked through the mess and went right for my bedroom and shut the door. For the next hour, I rested in bed, ignoring the music as best as possible, hoping I'd succumb to exhaustion.

Abruptly, what felt like deep sleep was interrupted by a strange noise. It was very dark in my room. I glanced over to my roommate's bed. It was empty. My alarm clock read 3:15 am. The music and the party were still alive. *Why did I awaken?*

Then it dawned on me. *3:15 am. Exactly one year ago.*

I saw my family circled around my dad, surrounded by machines. The beeping slowing down and then coming back again with disappointing hope that life was still possible. His bedsheets moving up and down with his last breaths. I felt right there again. The clock on the wall read 3:15 am. My chest began to tighten. My body wanted to rock.

I got up and locked the bedroom door. I wanted help, but not from a roommate who wasn't sober. Memories surrounded me. Being in the bathroom alone. Seeing Aunt Barbara and Uncle Bill at the end of the hall. Aunt Janice walking toward me with tears streaming from her eyes. My mom's brown leather purse. Where everyone stood in the room. The clock on the wall, ticking as my dad's last moments slipped away.

I closed my eyes, searching for something else to think about, but nothing could bust through the thoughts. I wasn't anywhere close to sleep, my mind flashing as fast as the first responders' red, white, and blue lights. I wanted it to stop, but I didn't know how. I needed help.

I looked at the phone. Even though I knew she would have understood, I didn't want to call my mom. It was really late and I wondered if she was going through her own *3:15 am*. If not, I didn't want to bring her there with me. I called a friend from college who tended to be a night owl, knowing he'd totally understand if I called him in the middle of the night. I had confided everything to him.

"Hello?" he said groggily.

"Hi, it's Susie," I said trying to hold back tears.

"Susie, what's wrong?" Immediately, he was concerned.

"I'm not doing so well." The tears I'd been holding back with every effort flowed.

"What do you mean?"

"It's the anniversary right now. I wanted to sleep through it, but I woke up and I can't stop thinking of everything. I can't stop thinking about the hospital and my dad passing and everything." Tears grew to sobs.

"Oh my god! That's terrible!"

"And my roommates are having a party and I can't stand hearing that right now . . ."

BEEP BEEP . . . you have one minute left.

Back then, the only way to call out on a landline at Disney was to use a calling card. If someone was calling the apartment from outside of the complex, they had to call the complex's main line and then the director would connect the person using an extension. This was not automatic and hours for receiving calls were limited. Definitely there was no one on duty transferring calls at 3:15 am.

"What was that?" he asked.

"That's my calling card. Shit, I don't think I have much time left on it."

"Do you have another card?"

BEEP BEEP . . . you have less than one minute left.

"No, I don't have another card!"

"Can you go get one?"

"I tried yesterday but the machine was broken, and I don't want to walk over there now."

BEEP BEEP.

"Oh god, I'm running out of time!"

"I don't know what to do. I don't know how to help you."

"I just need a friend! That's all I need right now!! I just need someone to listen . . ."

BEEP BEEP . . . your time is up. Click.

The party blared in the background. I began to rock, my arms folded in front of me, as usual without even realizing it. I couldn't stop. It was feeling so good again and releasing the tightness in my chest. I double checked that the bedroom door was locked. I didn't want anyone seeing me rock. I rocked for an hour until my energy ran out. It was exactly how I did not want to spend the first anniversary.

I OPENED MY EYES to bright sun illuminating the green trees outside the window and my roommate's bed still empty. I rubbed my eyes and glanced at my alarm clock. 7:00 am. I was exhausted and emotionally drained. *Aunt Barbara watching me sleep. Gayle coming in through the screen door. Hearing her crying with my mom in her bedroom.* This left me a mess. I needed a shower.

I got up, unlocked the bedroom door and headed for the bathroom, not making any attempt at remaining quiet for my roommates. In the shower, I spent a half hour trying to wash off the night before, wanting everything to go down the drain, until I couldn't stand my pruned fingers. I had no plan for the day except to get out and do anything other than be in the apartment with my roommates. After getting dressed, I headed for the living room where I was met with the biggest mess yet. I hated this. I hated them.

I hated the party. Walking around garbage, I opened the fridge hoping to find orange juice with my name on it. The carton was empty in the fridge.

"Hey, why did you lock the door?"

I jumped, not expecting to see my roommate that shared the bedroom with me lying on the couch.

"I'm sorry," I offered. "It must have been an accident." *An accident.* It stung a little that she didn't ask how I was, as if the story I shared at the beginning of the summer was long forgotten, which I have no doubt that it was by her and probably the other roommates.

Another roommate emerged from her dark bedroom wearing sunglasses, her uniform, and clearly the remnants from the night before. "I can't believe I have to go to work. I have the worst hangover," she griped.

"But it was a good party," my other roommate said as she glared at me. I turned away and searched the fridge for something that came close to resembling food that I could have for breakfast.

"Oh my god, can you believe that guy."

"I know! I can't believe he got in here! He must have hopped the fence."

That caught my attention. Our apartment was in a gated complex that housed only college interns for Disney. Even so, we were told from the beginning to report suspicious people. Rumors swirled that a few months before, someone had climbed over the fence, broken into someone's apartment, and raped two girls.

"What are you talking about?" I asked.

"Oh my god, Susie," my roommate exclaimed as she took off her sunglasses. From the looks of her bloodshot eyes, I don't know how she got out of bed. "You would not believe what happened! First of all, you missed a great party."

"Yeah, it was great," the other chimed in, still scowling at me.

"I came back over here to get more beer and as I was walking across, this big guy we'd never seen before came out of nowhere and asked if we had any beer."

I was alarmed. "Really?"

"Yeah, like a guy who clearly wasn't part of the college program . . . an old guy, like in his thirties or something . . . a totally creepy guy wearing worn-out clothes with a tattoo on his arm of a spider web. I had a beer in my hand when he asked if we had any beer, so I didn't really know what to say to him."

The other one snorted. "That's so funny!"

"I know," she said, laughing. "I mean, what was I going to say? No, I didn't have any beer?"

Both were laughing now.

"So I told him, 'Uh, yeah, we have beer,' and the next thing I know he's following me into our apartment. So he comes in and he's, like, looking around and he's like, 'Some party you've got going on,' and I had no idea what to say to him at all." She continued laughing like this was the funniest thing.

"So I give him a beer and he then tells me that he doesn't want a beer, and I'm like . . ., *Okay . . . what does he want?* and then I realize exactly what he wants, and I'm thinking, like . . ., *Oh shit.*"

My heart began to pound.

"So he picks me up, and as he's picking me up I'm so drunk that I'm thinking, like, *Why the heck am I in the air right now? Oh my god,*" they both laughed hysterically. "And he puts me down on the stool, so I'm standing on the stool."

"He put you on the stool?" I asked, trying to make sense of what I was hearing.

"Yeah, and then he starts fingering me." They are both nearly rolling on the floor laughing. "And I'm like, *Holy crap, he's actually fingering me.*"

More laughter.

"He's got his finger up my vagina, and I'm like, *Oh my god, like, what is he doing?!* And I haven't even lost my virginity yet!"

"And then I happen to walk in," the other one says, "and I'm, like, I can't believe what I'm seeing. I'm seeing this big guy with his hand up her skirt. He looked like he just got out of prison!"

"I know! The look on your face was priceless."

"No! The look on your face was priceless!" They both laughed. "I'm like, 'Hey, do you want to go back over to the other party?' and you're, like, just looking at me with these wide eyes and you just were . . . like . . . nodding yeah."

My stomach turned. "So did the guy leave?" I asked.

"Yeah. When she came in and asked if I wanted to go back to the boys' apartment, he then just wandered out. It was too funny!"

Then it dawned on me . . . the noise last night . . . the reason I woke up from the deep sleep in the first place. It was hard to ignore the *what if*.

"So when he left, did you lock the door?" I asked.

"Uh, no," one responded, as if stating the obvious. "We were still going back and forth between apartments."

It took everything inside of me not to punch her. What stopped me was knowing if I did so I'd never be able to work for Disney again. Anger grew, pushing the limits of the boundaries of the bubble that burst more times in the last year than in my entire lifetime. I didn't want it to happen again. I took a huge, deep breath. "I'm glad you're okay. From now on, the door always stays locked."

I left the apartment and didn't come back until early that night, when I knew they would all be out again, drinking, partying, and doing whatever, all so I could avoid seeing them and feeling rage.

MY AFTERNOON NAP was interrupted by the phone ringing next to my bed. I had worked an early shift and come back to an empty apartment, or so I thought. I only had three more days of work before the college program was over, and then I would pack up and go back to New Jersey to see my mom and get ready for my senior year at Syracuse. The summer felt like a success, but I dreaded going back to school. Taking a nap was one way to avoid thinking about it.

My strategy worked until the phone rang. Rather than answer it, I let the call go to the answering machine. After the incoming message played, I heard a click. "Hello?" answered one of my roommates. I thought I was home alone.

"Hi!" It was another roommate.

The answering machine recorded and blasted out this conversation next to me in my bedroom.

"Sorry I didn't pick up the phone. I was expecting Susie to get it since she's right next to it, but she's taking a nap and couldn't get herself out of bed to answer the fucking phone."

"Oh my god, she is so annoying."

"I can't believe she didn't come to that last party or go out with us last night."

"I know, right?!?! She's twenty-one!"

"I know! Like, she's not normal."

"She isn't. Whatever. She can kiss my ass."

"Exactly, she can . . . "

Then in unison . . .

"KISS MY ASS!"

I waited for my roommate to leave. As soon as I heard the front door shut, I got moving. In less than twenty minutes, I had all of my things packed up and in my car, ready to go. I called Margaret, a coworker who had become a good friend.

"Hello?"

"Hi Margaret. It's Susannah."

"Susanne-Susannadanna!" as she'd often call me. "What's up?"

"Can I stay at your apartment for three nights?"

"Sure! What's wrong?"

"I just need to get out of here. I'll explain later."

I didn't see any of the roommates after that. My empty drawers and stripped bed were my way of saying good-bye to them.

MARGARET AND I SPLIT a bottle of white zinfandel as I told her what happened. She had grown up in the backwoods of Florida. Like most of my coworkers, she didn't have a college degree. She worked very hard to earn a living, often juggling expenses while figuring out the next step in life. She was young, only two years older than me, but she was a responsible adult living a responsible life on her own without the help of her parents. She had been independent since she was sixteen.

"Man, those girls are complete idiots," she said in her perfect southern accent. "It's amazin' that they're in college. How can people in college be so stupid?"

I didn't defend them.

"I mean, jeez . . . Here yer just tryin' to work hard and be responsible and do the right thing after everythin' ya been through and these stupid girls have to be so mean to ya."

I took a sip of wine. "Yeah."

"Man, they have no idea what the world is all about. They're going to get chewed up and spit out." Margaret had a way of telling it like it is.

"I told you about the whole groceries thing, right?"

"Yeah, about how ya had to figure out how to put all of that milk in the dang fridge and they ended up just drinkin' each other's anyway. So stupid! And that one who actually laughed about that guy comin' in and fingerin' her! I mean, what kind of a dummy is she?"

My sips turned into guzzles. "Most of them were virgins."

Margaret looked at me, confused.

"I mean, it's not a big deal or anything," I explained. "It's just clear they didn't have much life experience."

"Well, one of 'em is a lil' less virgin now," Margaret noted.

I nearly snorted my wine.

Margaret had quite a life story already by the age of twenty-three. She grew up like a stray cat from a feral colony with a combination of poverty, neglect, and abuse. She left home with hardly anything except a strong desire for something better. She had very little money, but would give loans to friends all the time to help them out, believing that in life we're all in this together. Despite her past, she always thought positively. How we found common ground I'm not sure, but I was grateful we became friends. Our stories could not have been more different.

"Ya need to have more fun, though," she finally told me.

I knew that. Rejection from my roommates wasn't what bothered me. It was the reminder that despite my achievements, I had missed out. "Yeah," I acknowledged with a deep breath. "I know."

She poured me another glass of wine. "But at least yer not stupid!"

THE NEXT DAY WE BOTH went to work. Margaret and I made a point of making sure we had our lunch break together. I found her at a table with her usual hamburger and french fries, reading the cast member newsletter, a weekly publication that included articles about other employees, new company development, and internal job openings. Just as I sat down, she asked, "What ya think about this?" She pointed to a job listing for a low-level coordinator position in another park.

"You could do that," I encouraged. Margaret had the same job as me working as a hostess and buffet worker.

"Yeah, but I don't know if they'll even look at me. Look," she said pointing to the listing again, "it says resume required. I ain't got that!"

"That's no big deal," I explained. "You have a computer?"

"Yeah."

"Then tonight we'll write your resume."

Margaret laughed. "What am I gonna put on a dang resume? Hostess? Parked cars? Told people when they could go down the water slide?"

This remark bummed me out. As confident and strong as Margaret had come across to me, and as generous as she was with me and so many of her friends, it hit me that she didn't think she was worthy. "You've got nothing to lose. We'll write your resume tonight and we'll see what happens."

She sat back in thought. After a big sigh, "Okay. Guess we'll see. But read that job listin' again. Make sure ya know it so we get this thing here right."

I knew we could just as easily take the newsletter back to her apartment with us after work, but as I appeased her and reread the job description, something caught my eye.

Job opening - Assistant Casting Director full-time position for casting shows, management and organization skills required, theater experience a plus, must recognize good talent, call to set up an interview.

I read it again. *Full-time position. Assistant Casting Director. Theater experience a plus.*

"Margaret, check this out." I showed her the ad.

Without needing to explain further, she knew what I was thinking. "Wow, go fer it! You could do that job! Like ya just told me . . . What d'ya got to lose?" she exclaimed.

What I wanted was right in front of me. Immediately, I saw myself driving to and from work in my white convertible enjoying the Florida warmth. Palm trees, beautiful sunsets, weekends at the beach. A steady paycheck with benefits would support me comfortably in my modest apartment with a small balcony, where I would sit and enjoy a glass of wine. Work would be fun. I'd be watching talented actors perform and placing them in the right roles. My circle of friends would grow and I'd host dinner parties. Family and friends would come down to visit, and I'd get to show them around Disney. A dreamy life in my mind, until other thoughts crept in.

"Are ya gonna apply?" Margaret asked, waiting for my response, watching the wheels spin in my head.

Margaret sensed my doubt. "At least go for the interview! The worst that could happen is they say no!"

It was the worst that could happen. The interview alone would be a great experience, but getting the job and being frozen by doubt felt more devastating that not even trying at all. Or so I thought at the time . . . until I was driving back to New Jersey, overflowing with regret.

CHAPTER 4

Trapped in Syracuse

ASSIGNMENTS . . . SCHEDULES . . . Books . . . All seemed pointless except for the fact that if I passed two more semesters I would earn my bachelor's degree. On paper this would look great, but I questioned if it had any more worth than the paper it would be printed on. What was a sunny vision in Florida was far from reality. There was no paycheck. There were no birds of paradise. There wasn't even the answer to the *what if? What if I had interviewed?* It left me wondering. Because I didn't go for it, because I succumbed to fear, now I felt like an animal stuck in a small cage. Trapped by requirements. Trapped by a schedule. Trapped by snow . . . lots and lots and lots of snow.

I loaded up on classes for no good reason expect to distract myself from thinking about tropical weather. While at the annual party that kicks off the semester in the theater department someone told me that my friend Kimmy needed a stage manager for her show. I signed on, wanting the experience, but not fully realizing that stage managing a show in college is like an unpaid full-time job in that it requires keeping track of every moving part. My eighteen-hour days started with classes and ended with the show, and whatever free time was available in between these obligations was quickly filled with studying and grabbing a bite to eat. I didn't go to another party until the end of the semester. I didn't even go out to a bar.

Every time I went home to my apartment I collapsed into the black leather bean bag chair wondering what it would have felt like if that chair had a view of a palm tree instead of a gray sky.

To add insult to injury, only one week into the semester I was reminded that bad storms weren't only found in Florida.

Thankfully, I lived in a brick building, a school house that had been converted to condos. I rented a two-bedroom unit with a friend. The front door was unusually wide, as if it once was the school's music room—the bigger door possibly allowing a piano to be moved in and out. It was an extremely nice apartment by college student standards, with large windows and high ceilings and a living room/dining room combination big enough for a huge sectional, a big coffee table, two desks, and a dining table that sat six. I had a walk-in closet the size of my freshman dorm room. I also had a gated parking space, a luxury since the only other option was street parking, which was occasionally hard to come by. It was also less than a five-minute walk to the theater and campus and the rent was obscenely low. I was lucky to have found it after I lost my campus housing during my semester off; and even more so on the stormy night that was to come.

My roommate had left earlier that evening to hang out at a friend's house around the corner. She invited me to join her, but I chose to stay home, having heard earlier in the day that a bad storm was on its way. I hid the truth behind my decision by saying I was too tired. Once she left, I turned on the TV and didn't turn my attention away from it. The storm was about two hours away.

With each passing report, the meteorologists warned that the storm was gaining strength and would continue its momentum. The news didn't talk about anything else. I didn't move, wanting to know everything that was happening as it was about to unfold. Reports showed the radar over and over again, a large, thick red line was sweeping through Upstate New York. I imagined everything in its path blowing sideways.

The warnings grew in intensity. Higher wind speeds. Faster track. Larger hail. Meteorologists sweating, clearly concerned by what was unfolding, one practically screaming to get inside immediately. My heart pounded. I wondered if I was safe in this brick building.

I grabbed a flashlight from the kitchen drawer, hoping we wouldn't lose power. While heading back toward my bedroom, I noticed the stereo in the living room. It had a radio, which I turned on just in case we lost cable. Both the TV and the stereo blared weather reports. I headed back to my bedroom and through the tall windows noticed the leaves blowing in the wind. It wasn't a strong wind, but it was enough that after glancing at the TV and seeing the red line on the radar move closer and closer, I no longer felt safe in my bedroom. I moved into the hallway between my bedroom and the living room, as far as I could from the windows, but close enough that I could still hear the weather reports. I gripped the flashlight in my hand.

The hollow sound of garbage cans tumbling in the street jolted me. I didn't want to hear it. I wondered if everything was going sideways, the leaves clinging to the branches as they arced from the force. I wondered if it was here. Thunder rattled the building, the loudest I'd ever heard, putting the Florida storms to shame. I heard the rain pounding against the windows. I noticed myself rocking without even realizing. I stopped myself and curled up into a ball.

After a few minutes, the sounds outside quieted. I got up and went into my bedroom to check the radar. The screen was black. As I got off my bed to head into the living room to listen to the stereo, everything else went black. Immediately I sat on the corner of my bed, stiff and scared to move, tears filling my eyes.

More sounds. The howl of the wind. Rain crashed against the windows. Thunder made everything jump. *A thousand cardboard boxes . . .* the one sound I didn't actually hear, but knew someone else must be hearing it. Everything grew louder and louder. I rocked on that corner of the bed, even though it made me feel crazy, but it was the only way my pounding heart felt soothed. I didn't want to go backward, I didn't know what else to do but allow my body to do what instinctually it felt like it needed to do to survive. Stopping felt like my heart would explode.

The lights flickered on. The stereo clicked, the broadcast breaking the diminishing sounds outside. It had passed. It was 1:30 am.

My roommate strolled in. "Hey," she said.

I stopped rocking and jumped up from my bed. With a smile on my face, I greeted her with a "Hi!" that had more enthusiasm than I intended.

"Wasn't that storm crazy?" she asked.

As if it were no big deal, I replied, "I had the stereo on the whole time. All they talked about were the warnings. It sounded really bad. We lost power for a moment."

"I left because they lost power and I saw our building had lights on. I figured I'd come home."

As she said this, it dawned on me that she walked the short block outside during the storm, the same short block that's lined with large trees with big branches. "You walked home during the storm?" I asked sharply.

"I did for a little bit," she said as she set her bag down. "The wind was something!"

Concern I couldn't cover, "You couldn't wait for the storm to be over?"

She took a step back from me. "Well, it was just around the corner. It wasn't like I was far."

You could practically see the house she was at from our building. She likely left after the worst of the storm. Still, not wanting to know someone else who was hit by a tree, but not wanting to reveal that the storm affected me in any way, shape, or form, I said to her, "I'm just glad you're home safe. Next time, I don't think it's a good idea for you to walk around in a storm."

Her eyes widened. I had told her the story. I wasn't sure if she put two and two together, but I didn't want her to say it out loud. "Aww, that's so sweet," she smiled. "Thank you for thinking about me! I won't do that again." She hugged me and went to her bedroom.

I stayed up and listened to the weather reports.

CLASSES WERE CANCELLED for a few days because of damage from the storm. Power lines draped the streets and sidewalks, hung like Christmas lights on broken trees. Many of the large, old trees that dotted the quad on campus were no longer upright, their roots stretching so high and far that you could walk under them without needing to duck. Windows were blown out of dorm rooms. The brick facade of a building just blocks away now sat in a crumbled pile, exposing bedrooms, dressers, tables, and couches. Students were injured. Some reported being picked up and slammed down into the ground by the wind while walking outside. Those who were brave enough to look outside while the storm approached said the sky had turned bright green, followed by the strongest gust of wind some had ever felt.

Three people had died in the storm. Three families, without any warning, were now different. I wondered if any of them witnessed their loved ones passing, if they heard sounds that haunted them. I wondered if anyone rocked.

It took weeks to clean up the debris and restore full power. Walking to class, it was impossible to avoid seeing the storm's evidence. It was a frequent topic on TV and in the newspapers and conversation. It made me wish even more I had never left Florida.

ABOUT HALFWAY INTO the semester, the phone rang as I was typing an email on the computer. I reached for it, "Hello?"

"Hi, Susie. Uh . . . how are you?"

It was one of my roommates from Florida, the one whose life seemed breezy despite everything she'd been through. I nearly hung up, but curiosity rose. "I'm good," I hesitated. "How are you?"

"Uh, I'm good too. Listen . . . um . . . I know this is weird, but it was just really weird how you left and I feel really bad about that."

I didn't know what to say, so I stayed silent.

"And . . . uh . . . well, I talked to my mom about it and I vented to her about how much of a bitch you were and how come you couldn't hang out with us and then you just leave completely without saying good-bye ... "

I almost hung up.

"... and then my mom tells me how insensitive we all were and how badly we were treating you. You'd been through so much and she thought it was awful that none of us could give you any kind of compassion at all. She told me that we must have done some things that were so bad that you felt like you had to leave that way."

I couldn't believe what I was hearing.

"So, I just wanted to say that I'm really sorry, and I know the other girls are sorry too."

It was nice to hear the apology, but not wanting to get stung, I kept my wall up. "I accept your apology, but if the other girls want to apologize, I have to hear it from them."

"I understand," she replied. "I just don't want you to hate me."

I was surprised that she cared about how I felt about her. My anger and other issues took a lot away from me. I thought she was so lucky to be able to walk this life so carefree and relaxed, yet this unresolved thing between us that we never spoke about weighed on her. Rather than drag her down with me, I let it go. "Listen, maybe learn from this, but don't be so hard on yourself. You're lucky. You have no idea what it's like and you couldn't relate. Now let it go and move on."

"So you forgive me?" she pleaded. "I feel really bad."

"I think you should just move on. I have. You and the other girls should too." After saying that, my breath felt easier, something I didn't know felt heavy five minutes before. "Just do one thing though," I added.

"What's that?"

Another easier breath. "Be more compassionate to others. You never know what people are battling even when everything looks okay."

"I will. I'm so sorry," she said. "I just want you to know that I think you're a really cool person. That's why we all wanted to hang out with you."

Acknowledgment that she actually liked me . . . another reminder that I had missed out. "It's okay. Just move on. Enjoy the rest of your semester."

"Okay, you too."

I never heard from the other girls, but I was okay with that.

DURING WINTER BREAK restlessness settled in. Thoughts of Florida, wondering what the last few months would have been like if I had gotten the job and stayed there. No assignments and exams. No classes. No snow. No Labor Day storm . . . the irony was not lost on me that a major reason I didn't pursue the job was because I didn't think I could handle storms in Florida. I felt disappointed in myself for letting fear take over, for not dealing with it. I felt like I failed.

I couldn't allow myself to fail twice. Only one more semester and I'd earn my degree, which I'd been told all my life a college degree would open doors, although which doors I often wondered. Lucky for me, I only needed twelve more credits to graduate and nine of them needed to be applied to the Drama/Acting requirement. The other three credits could be in anything.

The thought of performing made me cringe. In high school I was able to memorize a two-page monologue for a production of a Greek tragedy in a half hour. Now, I couldn't even remember a short, four-sentence monologue as a favor for a friend who was a directing major and needed an actor for a scene for her class assignment, despite reading the piece several dozen times. The Drama Department offered two movement classes that would give me six credits. I signed up for both of them, remembering that movement classes were usually very fun, creative, and relatively easy; plus, they didn't require memorizing lines. Because the Drama Department emphasized being in good shape, physical education classes counted toward the Drama/Acting requirement.

In addition, I signed up for Self-defense for Women. It was a stretch, but technically it was a physical education class and the department accepted it. I rounded out my schedule with a Fine Arts class called Music in Film.

I spent my last semester in college doing yoga, dance, improvisational movement, pushups, situps, and punches, coupled with watching films while paying attention to the music. It wasn't palm trees and tropical air, but my classes made hiking up the hill through several feet of snow less miserable. After a few weeks of feeling sore and stiff, my body started growing strong muscles in my arms, legs, and abs. I was more physically fit than I'd ever been in my life.

We did a lot of yoga in one of my movement classes. I had taken up yoga a few years before after one of my acting teachers suggested it as a way of improving my posture. Back then I used a video tape with an hour-long routine and immediately fell in love. For a while I did yoga every day. I could feel muscle tension release with each stretch. I was amazed at how quiet and full my breath was at the end of the workout. My mind silenced. I felt centered. Before *a thousand cardboard boxes*, I had used yoga as a way of relieving stress. After, I stopped doing it.

Now, I was doing yoga again and it felt more powerful than ever. For the first time since I began my practice, I stretched into *adho mukha svānāsana*, also known as downward dog pose, and warmth poured down into my neck and shoulders. Every posture felt like a new awakening, like I was in a new body. I did all sorts of balance poses, ones I had never done before; even though these were challenging, the poses brought me to a place I hadn't experienced since in a long time. In a year and a half, I had gone from rocking and clutching my arms in front of my chest to arching my back into upward facing dog. *Ardha candrāsana*, or half-moon pose, made me feel like I was a hawk soaring through the sky. *Bālāsana*, child's pose, helped me rediscover inner peace.

Ironically, of all the balance poses that we did in class, the one that made me feel the strongest, most centered, and rooted to the floor was *vrksāsana*, also known as tree pose.

I gained flexibility and strength from practicing yoga, but more importantly and unbeknown to me, I began to shed the muscle memory my body held from *a thousand cardboard boxes*. These movements soothed me in a way rocking never could. Rocking was merely a Band-Aid for dealing with the pain. Yoga was a long-term solution.

The hours of exercise I did every day made my endorphins rush, but despite the positive effects, the easy schedule, and doing yoga, the regret of not making the phone call to get an interview for a job I knew I'd love in Florida ate at me. I felt trapped in snowy Syracuse in a holding pattern that prevented me from starting life in the real world. Even during the final weeks of the semester, I called my mom nearly every night, hoping she'd talk me into not quitting even though every fiber of my being wanted to jump in my car and drive a thousand miles south. She convinced me every time, reminding me that giving up on my degree would only lead to more regret.

To keep myself in Syracuse, I went back to the same pattern that kept me from rocking and believing I was okay: I busied myself. Classes. Assignments. A part-time job where I took extra hours every chance I could. I studied, even though Music in Film hardly required reading a textbook. No parties. No bars. No hanging out with friends.

The countdown to graduation crept closer. My focus remained laser sharp. Getting up every morning, going to class, going to work, always early, always doing my best . . . the things that I told myself I was supposed to do. Since a year and a half before I was rocking and couldn't remember how to fall asleep, to me going beyond basic functioning and handling responsibilities seemed like success.

It took me until then to learn the lesson that had screamed at me several times during the year, but that I chose to ignore. It had never occurred to me that maybe I wasn't succeeding until I was walking back from the library to my apartment one day late in the spring semester. It was a beautiful, sunny weekend and students played outside throwing Frisbees and laying out getting tanned. All of the windows and doors were open at the Greek houses along Walnut Avenue, music blasting from the mansions. It seemed like there were more kids outside than usual. Rather than join them, I went back to my apartment to work on the one paper I had to do for my Music in Films class.

It was an easy assignment, but I worked on it a lot. I got into the assignment, seeing if I could improve how I wrote the paper. It was the only paper I had to write the whole semester and it only needed to be ten pages long, yet I chose to immerse myself in writing it while ignoring the amazing weather and the last few days I had on campus as a college student.

The next day was equally beautiful. I was done with my paper. I didn't have to go to work. There was nothing I needed to do for my movement classes. I went to the grocery store, came home, and watched movies by myself.

While I was out, I noticed that there weren't nearly as many students outside as the day before. I figured everyone must have taken the one day to enjoy themselves and now they were inside scrambling to finish their papers and projects. I felt lucky to have completed my work, like I was smarter than everyone else for having been so diligent.

I was very wrong. Later in the day as I walked to Marshall Street to treat myself with takeout for dinner as a reward for all of my hard work, I saw groups of students together, many looking like they'd been in the sun all day. I wondered where they came from.

"That concert was the best!"

"I can't believe I saw them play! And it was free!"

"I wonder if MTV will come back next year?"

I noticed more students walking back toward the Greek houses and apartments, smiling, tanned, and tipsy, as they talked about this concert. Then as I turned onto M Street right in front of me I saw a flyer posted on the wall of a bar. MTV had brought a bunch of really hot bands for an all-day music festival on campus.

And I had missed it.

I got my takeout and went straight back to my apartment, fighting a lump that was building in my throat. The questions flowed through my mind. *Why did I not know about the concert? Why am I not going to parties? Why aren't I social? Why can't I be like everyone else? What is my problem?*

That question . . . *What is my problem?* What was it? Was this just me? Did I just like being this way? Was this who I was now? If that's the case, then why was I upset?

Why was I sad that I missed the concert? Why was I now sad that I missed parties? Why was I now sad that college was almost over and I hadn't made a ton of friends and done the things that college kids do?

But I'm dealing with it, I kept telling myself. *Functioning. I was doing what I was supposed to be doing... wasn't I?* I was getting good grades and working to support myself. *Isn't that what I'm supposed to be doing?*

Supposed. I questioned the importance I had put on that word, even though I hung on to it as a way to prevent me from rocking or spending the day in bed. What I was *supposed* to do. What was I really *supposed* to do? These kids that walked passed me smiling and laughing, most of them were getting their work done, some of them were going to graduate with honors, and maybe a few of them already had jobs lined up.

They were doing what they were supposed to do. They were living life.

I wasn't.

I remembered a story my dad told me about when he was in college and President Kennedy was assassinated. He and a few of his college buddies hopped into a car and drove from Gettysburg College down to Washington, D.C., with the goal of getting a glimpse of the funeral procession. They left the night before, knowing it would be a long drive and wanting the opportunity for the best view possible. It was still dark when they arrived, but during the drive, their plan evolved to hopping the fence at Arlington National Cemetery, climbing a tree as close to the burial site as possible, and waiting. They didn't realize that Secret Service would show up. My dad swore they saw them in the tree, but didn't do anything, perhaps believing they were kids who only wanted to pay their respects. Still, they didn't move for fear of losing their perfect view. They stayed there all day until midafternoon when the casket finally made its way past them. They watched the entire burial ceremony. They missed a day of classes . . . classes they were *supposed* to attend.

While other students were cramming for exams during the remaining few weeks until graduation, I crammed in as much fun as I could. Parties. Lunch with friends. Lying in the sun. Getting out. Laughing. Loving. Finding an adventure every day. My friends, some whom I only now began to form deep connections, told me how happy they were that I was out with them. This gave me a bittersweet feeling.

A unique celebration in the Drama Department is Marathon, an end-of-the-year party that starts in the theater and ends at Marathon House. Each senior has an opportunity to get on stage to sing a song, perform a monologue, say a speech, or do anything they want to do aside from getting naked, which happened once years before and caused quite the drama in the Drama Department. Performances range from the silly and outrageous to some of the best numbers I've ever seen. Afterward, everyone goes to a house a few blocks from the theater that is rented by Drama Department students with the understanding that they'll host the first and last parties of the year . . . and often many in-between. The dress code is anything goes, but most partygoers get fancy. I had splurged on a long, silky lavender gown that reeked of old Hollywood glam. It required jewelry, so naturally I had to get that at my favorite boutique on M Street, the one where everything was way out of my price range and where I'd occasionally find something affordable on the sale rack.

I also needed help with my long hair, so I asked Jackie for help. She was a popular hair stylist on M Street, tall and blond, and as rumor had it, she'd possibly been "Jack" before Jackie, though I didn't know for sure. She was the epitome of glamour, having done hair for the Miss America Beauty Pageant. She invited me to her house for a pre-Marathon party where she spent over an hour getting my hair into the most amazing French twist adorned with pearl and crystal accessories. After I did my makeup and got dressed, Jackie gasped. "You are such a star!" I loved hearing this although I knew I'd never be a movie star and never perform on a stage again. This was my final opportunity to look and feel like one. When it came to be my turn on stage, I chose to be myself.

"You look beautiful!" shouted a junior who sat at the side of the stage ready to hop on the piano at the request of many seniors. A few whistles followed. I

PEACE WITH TREES

saw a sea of smiles. Considering that I had been in a cocoon for most of my junior and senior years and didn't do any shows as I tiptoed through the remainder of my program, I was sure half the room didn't know who I was. Either way, the love that radiated from the audience was the strongest I'd ever felt.

"Nearly two years ago, I lost two things . . . ," I started, "my dad and my love for theater."

The theater silenced.

"I am very fortunate that only one of these things was temporary."

I showed off that despite taking a semester off I managed to graduate on time with honors, but I came clean, admitting that I had no idea what I was going to do, but I was ready to trust that whatever I would do would be right for me. I told them about the times I called my mom wanting to quit, knowing she would stop me. Then I read a poem about how when things go wrong one should never give up.

On the way to the party, two friends approached me at two different times, both with tears in their eyes. It seemed that I struck a chord in them with what I said. It made me realize that even though I was the only one who experienced *a thousand cardboard boxes*, I wasn't alone in feeling pain and fear. Perhaps I wasn't as different as I thought I was from everyone else.

Despite the celebration of earning our degrees, the undercurrent of *now what* seeped through. As I made my way to the party with a bottle of white zinfandel in hand, I wondered where we would all land. The common question nearly every senior got from underclassmen—"What's next?"—was usually answered with a comment like "Another beer."

That question lingered while packing my belongings, putting on my graduation cap, opening congratulatory cards, and hugging friends goodbye. *Now what?*

CHAPTER 5

Roommates

MY MOM AND I LOOKED BACK and forth between the instructions and the power washer, trying to make sense of what we believed was an easy thing to use. We thought we had it down, but when my mom turned it on only a tinkle of washer fluid came out. It was my bright idea to power wash and seal the deck, even though I'd never lived in a house with a deck before, yet somehow I knew they needed power washing and sealing. It was the beginning of the first summer in my mom's new house, or rather her new-to-us house.

We moved in together. My mom invited me back, emphasizing that I could save money. It wasn't a difficult decision given that my measly income barely supported the two-bedroom apartment in the Journal Square section of Jersey City I'd been sharing with two roommates. I got that apartment with a few friends shortly after graduating college, again falling into the trap of doing what I believed I was *supposed* to do, even though I had no plan, a part-time retail job that was closer to my mom, and a nonpaying internship at a documentary production company on the Upper East Side. Both jobs sucked money out of my account in gas, train, and subway costs. There was even a week where I had only a dime to my name.

I remembered a TV program about Madonna's career path of moving to Manhattan and only eating popcorn to survive. After eight months of balancing change, dodging parking tickets, and sweet-talking my landlord into accepting my portion of the rent late without a penalty, I realized the obvious: Madonna and I were not the same.

Just as I was about to move out of Jersey City, my mom began house hunting. Even though our yellow farmhouse was where *a thousand cardboard boxes* took place, it was hard to leave. It was a home filled with memories I could recall in a heartbeat. The time I roller-skated around the dining room table and it tipped over and fell on my hand. The time my parents hosted a PTA barbecue where way more people showed up than expected, and Gayle and I spent the afternoon upstairs in my bedroom after we walked into our small playroom and saw about twenty kids playing with, and damaging, our toys. The time I picked two large baskets of green beans from the garden. The time when Mickey snuggled with me on the couch when I was sick. The time I opened my acceptance letter to Syracuse University and my mom and I made a poster to hang on the porch for my dad to see as he came home from work. The homework times. The dinner times. Sleepovers. Holidays. Waiting for the school bus. My beautiful childhood. That was the home where it had all unfolded. A place I thought would always be happy.

It also became a home where I forced myself out of bed. A house where we pretended everything was fine on the first Christmas after, even though as we gathered in the living room no one wanted to sit in the blue Ethan Allen chair that was by far the most comfortable option. A house whose floors creaked less, whose walls didn't echo laughter, whose refrigerator wasn't as full. The grass wasn't as manicured. The garage missed a car. The closets held hangers without clothes.

Mickey knew it was different, opting to sleep more, probably knowing the big guy who grilled him his own hamburger and snuck him a slice of American cheese while watching TV from the recliner was no longer here. He became thinner. At first we thought it was from not eating hamburgers and American cheese, until the vet told us otherwise. It wasn't until I left early one morning to go to the city for my documentary internship that I glanced into my mom and dad's bedroom and saw Mickey sleeping on his favorite blue blanket on the bed, the side where my dad slept. He wasn't curled up like usual. I walked toward him. He didn't raise his head and purr as he normally did. He looked at me with sadness in his eyes.

"Hang on for a little bit for me," I whispered to him. I had to catch the train, hoping my internship would turn into something, not wanting to miss a day or an opportunity. A few hours later, the knots in my stomach grew so big I couldn't ignore them. I left early, fearing that day might be the day for Mickey.

When I got home, he was in the same position. I petted his head gently. He responded with a long meow that sounded like "It may be time and I'm sorry."

"Okay," I whispered as I kissed his forehead. "It's going to be okay."

We immediately went into an examining room when we arrived at the vet's office. He pulled him out of the carrier.

"Yeah, I can see he's lost some fluids," he showed me. As he lifted Mickey's tail, I saw that his belly and rear were soaked. "We'll put him on an IV and see what we can do."

As the vet turned him over, Mickey perked up. He looked at me, his eyes no longer sad. He looked alert, like maybe he realized he was wrong, that now was not his time. I didn't say goodbye. I came home to a message that he crossed over the rainbow bridge the moment I left.

My mom was ready for a change. It wasn't long after Mickey passed that my mom heard from a friend that a couple was interested in our house. After several months of house hunting, my mom found her perfect home in Boonton, New Jersey: a turn-of-the-century colonial on a postage stamp-sized property and with a humongous pine tree overtaking the majority of the front yard. My mom had that tree cut down the week she and I moved in.

Mom had many more plans for the house besides removing the tree. Every room was painted, every surface of wood sanded and refinished or painted. Even the siding and windows were replaced. She shopped for fabric and made all of the window treatments herself. After work and weekends, she sanded, painted, weeded, planted, cleaned, sewed, furnished, and decorated nearly nonstop until it was what she wanted. She had always kept a clean house and garden, but I'd never seen her roll up her sleeves quite like this with such determination and passion. Even on the nicest of weekends, she stripped, sanded, and stained the double-sized pocket door that led into the dining room, bringing it back to its original condition. Before any of these projects began, my mom proudly welcomed her friends over to show off her new home and many had the same reaction: "It's so Sally!"

My mom beamed every time she heard those words. She made it her own by spending days hand stenciling a border around the dining room . . . *Home! Sweet Home!* by John Howard Payne.

Mid pleasures and palaces though we may roam,
Be it ever so humble, there's no place like home;
A charm from the skies seems to hallow us there,
Which seek thro' the world, is ne'er met elsewhere.

A charm from the skies seems to hallow us there was my favorite line.

But on the day we both struggled to make sense of the directions for the power washer, it didn't feel like anyone was *hallowing* us from anywhere. Feeding off my mom's sense of independence from purchasing her own home by herself and making it hers, never was there a house project that reminded me of my dad's absence until then. Not that he was always perfect when it came to following directions. I could remember spending two hours with him on our breezeway assembling a grill whose instructions came in broken English. Maybe because I was young, he had never let on about his frustration. Instead, we figured it out like a puzzle, feeling accomplished when it was completed, and perhaps a little stupid that it took us so long.

Just as I thought about the grill, my mom, drenched in sweat from having spent over an hour in the sun reading the directions, turned to me and said, "Does this remind you of the the time you and your dad had to put together the grill?"

I HAPPENED UPON a full-time retail job that took me to Sweden twice, once for six weeks in the winter and then the following summer for five weeks. It was everything a young twenty-something woman would want, or so I thought. It came with good things: high pay, full benefits, a 401(k) plan, and a daily cash allowance while abroad. The smokescreens of career happiness and excitement were in place: fashion, luxury hotels, and celebrities. While in Stockholm, days were spent working while nights were spent spending. Clubs. Drinks. Dinners. On my first night in Stockholm, a coworker who had been in Sweden training for over three months took a group of us to a new exclusive club called Kitchen. While sitting at the bar drinking a white zinfandel, a guy named Edvin told me he loved me while his friend made out with my coworker. Despite his advances, after many drinks and lots of dancing I went back to my hotel room alone.

More clubs, more dancing, more drinking. Nice restaurants. Shopping nearly every day. Being young and feeling free in an amazing European city with beautiful people. I didn't want to leave Sweden.

Had I known I'd be in a hot warehouse in Secaucus, New Jersey, for several weeks after returning from Sweden I would have missed my flight home on purpose. The glamor didn't return. Instead it was replaced by gossip, cattiness, bitchiness, and an unpredicted chaos that came with opening the first clothing store of a major worldwide company with so many customers packed between clothing racks that nothing stayed pretty. That only got worse.

Returning back to Sweden in the summer, thanks to a hard-earned job promotion, I anticipated returning to the excitement, only to be faced with a competitive environment. A handful of us were the first to be promoted and the realization that one of us could one day be country manager or in any other high-up position, made even simple conversations with colleagues calculated. Working and socializing together meant no escape, until a sign in a window of a spa near my hotel captured my attention. It was written in Swedish, but I knew it said massage.

I ignored it the first time. Every day leaving and returning from work, the sign caught my eye. It was only after a particularly vicious day at work that the sign seemed to scream at me, as if saying if I don't acknowledge it now, I might miss out on one of Sweden's greatest offerings: the Swedish massage. I went inside.

The woman behind the counter said I could make an appointment for a thirty-minute, sixty-minute, or ninety-minute massage. I chose the ninety-minute massage, figuring the longer the better. Four days later, I came back for my massage. When I made the appointment, I focused so much on understanding the receptionist that I didn't look around. It was a cute place, unexpectedly whimsical in what was a trendy neighborhood. The walls were lavender with painted flowers. Salon chairs and mirrors lined the room. It didn't match what I knew of Stockholm.

It cost the equivalent of $150, which felt easy to spend. The receptionist told me to come with her. I followed her across the room and through a doorway. We approached a flight of steps, steps that seemed like they led to a basement. I got a little nervous, wondering where she was taking me. At the bottom of the steps, we turned a corner and entered a white, cave-like basement. Celtic fabrics draped the walls and candles were everywhere—the only source of light. This is what I have come to understand is a typical basement in older Swedish buildings.

While in Gamla Stan, the older section of Stockholm, I once visited a coffee shop that had a street-level entrance that led down a long flight of steps into a similar basement with walls and arched ceilings. So many of these fabulous places in centuries-old buildings in Stockholm had unassuming entrances that led to these amazing basements, caverns connected by archways forming different rooms, giving you a feeling of hibernation and going within as you explored its hiding places.

We walked through the Celtic printed curtains and into a large room. The minute I entered, I knew I was in for something fantastic. A massage table in the center of the room sat very low, much lower than I thought it would, under it a colorful Moroccan rug. More candles illuminated the space, giving the cave a primal feel. The sounds of the ocean emanated from the walls as if an ocean was all around me. Amethyst and quartz crystals were scattered around the edges of the room, some very large, and all radiated a magnificent sparkle. A large Buddha sat on a side table draped with bright fuchsia Indian fabric. A faint smell of sandalwood incense burned. A wooden screen stood in one corner, presumably where I would get changed. In the opposite corner sat a young, tall, thin Swedish woman who wore yoga clothes and a thick, fabric headband. She was barefoot. She sat tall on a stool, writing in a journal as I entered the room. She did not speak English very well, so we introduced ourselves through the receptionist. Slowly and carefully, the massage therapist asked me if I had any tightness anywhere. I put my hands on my neck and shoulders and explained that I often got a lot of tension and that I had been under a lot of stress in the last few years.

"Okay," she acknowledged. "What is *stress?*"

Her question took me by surprise. *How do I explain stress?* I didn't want to explain everything. While I searched for words, she somehow seemed to understand. She asked me to get undressed behind the screen and to come to the table and lie face down.

I went behind the screen and undressed, feeling the coolness of the room. I made my way to the massage table, got face down, rested my head in a cushioned cradle, and felt a degree of warmth on the table I didn't expect. It was so comfortable. I let myself sink into it and released a deep, heavy breath. Something shifted even before the massage began. On the table, I felt more comfortable than I had in years. I stared at the Moroccan rug below me, wondering what was about to happen.

The next thing I knew, the massage therapist's hands glided down my spine like a dolphin diving into my back, accentuated by the sounds of the ocean. Perfect pressure. Warm hands. For ninety minutes, my mind savored every move she made. She spent a lot of time on my neck and shoulders, eventually whispering to me that I was very tight.

At the end of the massage, while lying face-up on the table and gazing at the arched ceiling, my breath was deeper than I ever thought possible. Complete relaxation, a new feeling to me. My mind was quiet and calm. No background noise. This state of mind was galaxies away from *a thousand cardboard boxes*. A new way of being, of breathing, of feeling, the layers of tension now stripped away. It was the most powerful therapeutic experience I had ever had. I felt back at the beginning, like a fresh start to a new me.

The massage therapist told me to get up slowly.

"That was incredible," I told her.

"*Tack*," she replied. *Thank you.* She seemed to understand.

I got up, moving slowly, exploring my new posture, new energy. After I dressed and emerged from behind the screen, I saw her sitting on her stool writing in her journal.

She looked so centered, so aligned with her purpose. She did this for a living, making people feel incredible, wearing yoga clothes, walking around barefoot, and writing in a journal . . . all for a living. She worked in a beautiful humanmade cave, surrounded by crystals, sandalwood, and ocean sounds. Seeing her made me want to do what she was doing.

A seed was planted. Eight months later, it grew into me quitting my job and going back to school for massage therapy, and then on to graduate school to study acupuncture.

THROUGHOUT SCHOOL, patterns remained. Up early, both me and my mom, finding our rhythm for sharing our one bathroom as we got ready for work. We breakfasted separately with the small TV in the kitchen on the local news. She often left first. I double checked that the house was locked before leaving. Returning from work, my mom cooked dinner and we ate together. I helped clean up afterward. We sat in the living room and watched *Jeopardy!* and *Wheel of Fortune*, usually followed by some show on HGTV. We spent weekends together doing things around the house, taking drives to Lafayette to look at antiques, and going on shopping trips. Our pattern was only slightly interrupted by the occasional dinner out with friends, many times both of us going together. Even when I met someone who became my boyfriend for five years, the pattern stayed mostly the same. Twenty-something and seeking friendship from my mom when I wasn't out on a date. Our relationship became that of friends. It seemed like a great situation.

Diagnosing Myself

I WAS FILLING OUT ACUPUNCTURE intake forms during one of my practical classes when it hit me. I was in my second year of school, which meant practicing our skills by treating each other, which required completing these forms.

Please list any surgeries, injuries, hospitalizations, and traumas.

I looked at that last word: *traumas.* It jumped out at me, because trauma was the category that meant the most. Physical or emotional pain, to me, were both important. While studying acupuncture, we learned how injuries, pathologies, and emotions can manifest in what acupuncturists term a *pattern of dishar-mony*. Anger, joy, worry, grief, and fear—and their nuances—all had different effects on the body.

A thousand cardboard boxes. I remembered chest pains and labored breathing while waiting at the hospital, at times feeling like I was on the verge of a heart attack. Rocking . . . a physical coping method for my emotional roller coaster with multiple highs and lows. The effects of my trauma were still there. Thunderstorms put me on edge, oftentimes keeping me from doing things like meeting up with friends. I dreaded the spring when they were more common, knowing that the first few storms made me very nervous.

As I pondered that blank space on the form, searching for a label, it came to me that I had post-traumatic stress disorder, PTSD. It made sense. I had witnessed a terrible event, and after that event I had a lot of stress, enough so that you could classify it as a disorder, if you would call social withdrawal and purposely avoiding storms a disorder. I didn't know much about PTSD, but I imagined anxiety and insomnia would fit the classification. It was the first time I had ever considered that there could be a diagnosis for what I had experienced in the past and still felt on some occasions.

I put down "PTSD due to an accident," even though this was a self-diagnosis and I didn't even know the definition of the disorder. Still, I knew without a doubt that *a thousand cardboard boxes* was imprinted into the fabric of my being, and since acupuncture treatments are geared toward releasing patterns, I was confident it would help in some way. We were going to be giving and receiving acupuncture treatments to each other for the next year and this was an opportunity to help me feel better, to possibly end the anxiety, nervousness, and heart palpitations that came with strong storms.

After two of my classmates, who were also my close friends, looked over the forms, they asked what I expected. "What do you mean by 'PTSD due to an accident'?"

"It's the biggest thing I've ever gone through. I witnessed an accident that ultimately took my dad's life."

An awkward silence followed as I waited for the next question, but it became apparent that my friends were stuck on finding the easiest, most gentle way of asking *what happened?*

"A storm came out of nowhere and a tree fell on him as he was coming in from getting the mail. He survived initially, but for thirty-five hours we didn't know what was going to happen, and during that time I experienced chest pains, very shallow breathing, and I rocked like a drug addict in withdrawal."

More silence, now uncomfortable. Then I continued to talk. "Since then, I feel on edge during storms. They make me nervous because of what happened. I've had moments where it was so bad that I've rocked to help ease the anxiety. I can't stand the spring because I know thunderstorms will start up again. I sometimes think of it as 'thunderstorm season.'"

Not wanting to keep talking, I hoped for some kind of response. As they stared back at me, still searching for what to say, it became clear to me that I was good at hiding this. For the two years we had spent together in class, socializing during lunch breaks and hopping around Manhattan whenever we got a chance, never had they suspected that on some occasions I suffered from tremendous anxiety, avoided storms like the plague, and rocked often without realizing that my body was moving.

"I just figured this was relevant," I explained, hoping this story wouldn't change things, that to them I was still their friend who always joined in whatever after-class activity was happening and who had a clear vision as to how I would build my acupuncture practice and who was overall very happy. It wasn't far from the truth. For the first time since *a thousand cardboard boxes*, I was happy . . . mostly. Driving through the Lincoln Tunnel at 8:00 am for an eight-hour class on a Sunday, every time I thought how exciting it was that I found a new dream and I was able to pursue it. Sometimes a month would go by before I had a day off from work and school, but that never bothered me. Between work and school I packed in time with family and friends. There were days where I'd be up early and wouldn't get home until well past midnight, sometimes for a few days in a row. Friendships were easier. Everything felt easier except storms.

Thunderstorms were the only things that were still hard. For example, after a night out with a group of coworkers at a local restaurant, the dark sky lit up just as we exited. As everyone else casually strolled to their cars, I hesitated at the door until a coworker jokingly asked me if I was planning to stay behind and wash dishes. I wouldn't have been surprised if I was the only one gripping the steering wheel during the twenty-minute drive to get home as my car got blown against by the wind and was pounded by rain.

Another time, while running out to grab lunch at our favorite sandwich shop just minutes from my workplace, a tall, thin tree toppled over from a rather light breeze just as I was walking in from my car. The sound wasn't as loud as the maple tree limb being wrenched off by the wind, perhaps only a hundred cardboard boxes, but my heart started to pound and my hands shook uncontrollably. While driving back to work, my eyes welled up.

August, a month that began with my dad's birthday on the first and ended with memories I didn't want to replay, was my least favorite month. Beautiful summer days where everything seemed still, just as they had on that morning, also reminded me.

I don't recall a wedding where the father of the bride didn't walk his daughter down the aisle. The crack of a ball hitting the bat at Yankee Stadium, a sound so distinct I could instantly think of my dad perking up with his eye on the ball, more focused on the game than I realized. Father's Day made me think of silk ties. Cadillacs made me think of how he held the steering wheel lightly with his left fingers at five o'clock.

"Do you have any other symptoms of PTSD?" they asked.

I didn't want to share any more than what I already had. They developed a treatment plan and got started. As they inserted the needles, I could tell they were focusing on my heart and pericardium organs. In acupuncture when we look for patterns of disharmony, many times these patterns relate to organs. Signs, symptoms, and physical evaluations bring information needed to paint a picture of disharmony, a pattern so to say, of how that person functions or dysfunctions. Many times, major illnesses, accidents, and surgeries, even if they occurred decades ago, need to be considered when forming a treatment. Even anything unusual at birth, such as being pulled out with forceps, makes an impact. From a Western medical perspective, my heart health was perfect: My blood pressure and cholesterol were always in the ideal range and my pulse rate was normal. Because I had chest pains during the trauma, my heart and pericardium were clearly affected. From an Asian medical point of view, the emotion associated with the heart and pericardium is joy, and for years after, I had a lack of joy. Also my posture wasn't the best. My shoulders often rounded forward and my chest slightly caved in as if I were physically trying to protect my heart.

The intellectual side of me as an acupuncture student wanted to stay alert and follow along with the acupuncture point selection. Then after the third needle was inserted, the other side of me wanted to give in. I closed my eyes and allowed myself to sink into the treatment. Warmth grew in my chest, my ribs relaxed, my breath deepened. I completely lost track of where needles were inserted. The noise from my other classmates in the packed clinic room seemed distant although we were separated only by thin privacy screens to form eight small separate treatment areas. The overhead lights appeared less bright. My body felt heavy. I reached an inner quiet and rested there.

The best part of an acupuncture treatment is the inner quiet it promotes. It's not always reached, and sometimes it's not as deep as we want, but every once in a while it's epic. I hoped this treatment would be one of those experiences. As I allowed the points to do their magic, one word kept repeating in my mind: *release*. I wanted the anxiety that came from storms and from thinking of *a thousand cardboard boxes* gone. *Release*. My sternum relaxed. *Release*. My breath sank even deeper. *Release*. Just as it felt like my heart opened a tiny bit, a rush of warmth passed through my body. What I once thought was relaxation was again redefined.

Just at the right time, when the noise in the room sounded a little louder, when the lights appeared a little brighter, I heard the squeak of the privacy screen between me and the next patient. "How are you doing, Susannah?" my classmate asked as he stepped into the treatment space.

"Amazing."

For that year in school whenever I had the opportunity after that, my heart was treated. As time progressed, my posture straightened, my shoulders relaxed back. My breathing felt easier, less restricted. I was calmer, more relaxed in general. As springtime approached, it seemed less alarming. When the first thunderstorm came, I noticed it and let it pass. I felt unaffected . . . and hopeful.

I decided to look up the definition of PTSD. According to *Taber's Cyclopedic Medical Dictionary*, it is defined as follows:

> *Intense psychological distress, marked by horrifying memories, recurring fears, and feelings of helplessness that develop after a psychologically traumatic event, such as the experience of combat, criminal assault, life-threatening accidents, natural disasters, or rape. The symptoms of PTSD may include re-experiencing the traumatic event (a phenomenon called "flashback"); avoiding stimuli associated with the trauma; memory disturbances; psychological or social withdrawal; or increased aggressiveness, irritability, insomnia, startle response, and vigilance. The symptoms may last for years after the event . . .*

Given that I had chest pains and a range of emotions and was rocking after the psychologically traumatic event, I would call that *intense psychological distress.*

In the beginning, I'd find myself thinking about flashing lights, wind, rain, responders, *a thousand cardboard boxes*. Were these *flashbacks*?

I recalled that I had wanted desperately for that tree to be taken down after the accident. I also avoided looking at or going through my dad's things. And then there were my nerves during storms with strong winds. Were these things *avoiding stimuli associated with the trauma*?

Memory disturbances . . . a thousand cardboard boxes.

I hardly hung out with friends or went to parties for the rest of the time I was in college after the accident. *Social withdrawal.*

There were also those times when I'd snap at people and get incredibly angry over the littlest of things. *Increased aggressiveness. Irritability.*

I didn't sleep well for at least a year after the accident. *Insomnia.*

If a storm was approaching, I absolutely had to be indoors and wait it out. *Vigilance.*

I'd had PTSD this entire time.

CHAPTER 7

Sea Glass

LONG AFTER ONE MOVES beyond grief, when stretches of time pass by where you don't think about the one who's gone, it's almost like you forget to remember them. Sometimes it's startling when you don't even remember the last time you thought about them. Then some moments practically smack you in the face and remind you that they're never gone. The first time I experienced this latter phenomenon was on a sand bar in Connecticut seven years after I lost my dad.

Uncle Bill and Susan had bought a second home on the Long Island Sound in Fairfield. It was a place for them to escape the concrete jungle of Manhattan, a place where friends and family could sunbathe on the lawn and throw fishing lines from the sea wall while enjoying a late afternoon gin and tonic. It was a popular place. Despite its four bedrooms and in-law suite, coming up for the weekend often required making a reservation, and sometimes even the second or third choice dates were unavailable. Who wouldn't want to spend the weekend in a gorgeous beachfront house with a gourmet kitchen, large living areas, vast water views, and the most important aspect of every weekend stay—Uncle Bill and Susan's ability to make the time spent together fun.

This was their dream home, the first one they saw when they went house hunting. As Uncle Bill would say: *It fit the bill.* It more than fit the bill. It became a gathering place for holidays, for escape, for memories. As excited as my whole family was when we first saw this house, a tiny part of me wondered if deep down Uncle Bill was sad that my dad wasn't here to enjoy it with us. If he hadn't passed, he would have spent nearly every weekend there with his brother fishing off that sea wall while sipping a Crown Royal on the rocks.

During one of my weekend getaway trips, I wasn't thinking about any of this. I went for a morning walk on the sand bar that stretched from a few houses east to a lighthouse that stood on a tiny island. Despite being called a sand bar, it was mostly made up of smooth stones and piles of shells. Seagulls often picked up various crustaceans in their beaks, flying up about twenty feet and then dropping them onto the rocks, using the force on impact to open the shells to feast on their prey. During high tide, the water of the Sound washed over the entire length of the sand bar, but during low tide many people walk along its path while admiring the view of Long Island and searching for treasures. On the previous morning's walk, as I was stepping off the sand bar to head back to the house, I encountered one woman who excitedly showed me her findings.

"Sea glass!" she exclaimed.

In her hand were three pieces of sea glass. Three different sizes and colors: one brown, one green, one clear. All had been weathered smooth from thousands of tumbles through waves and sand as jagged shards of broken glass to form matte bubbles of joy for her. It was as if she had plucked aquamarine from the side of a mountain in Colorado or a gold nugget from an old creek bed in Alaska. Her face beamed from her small collection of gems found within the tremendous path of stones and shells, perhaps because coming across sea glass was as challenging as finding crystals in mountains or because she found beauty from what was once broken.

Either way, as I began my walk on the sand bar, her treasures came to mind . . . along with my dad. *Hey, Dad, let's find some sea glass*, I thought.

We had never found sea glass together. As much time as we had spent on the beach down the Jersey Shore, we had never gone for a walk. Still, out of the blue after having had one of those long stretches of time where I forgot to remember, something inside me whispered to ask him. *Dad, let's find some sea glass.*

He was up for the task. Almost immediately, I looked down and saw a penny-sized piece of smooth green glass nestled among a ton of white shells.

WOW! I thought.

I took a few steps. *Let's find some more.*

Seconds later, wedged between other shells sat a dark brown piece, bigger than the green one. *You're really here, aren't you! Show me by finding more.*

Feet away from the brown one was another green piece. Next to it was a clear piece, nearly impossible to see against the dizzying pattern the white shells formed. After scooping them up, I took a few steps, and then felt a whisper to stop and look down. My eyes were guided to another brown piece. While bent over picking up the brown piece, my eyes were guided again, this time to my right about three feet. Another clear piece.

For three hours, we played this game. We found a rhythm: I walked until I felt the whisper, which drew my eyes downward as if directed to look at a specific spot. Sure enough, there was always a piece of sea glass. Some pieces weren't worn enough. *Sorry, Dad . . . I don't think that one counts.* Some were wedged so deeply between stones that they were nearly impossible to see. Some were even underneath shells and rocks, completely obstructed from view.

Before I knew it, both hands were full of glass. I shoved the pieces into the two pockets at my hips on my cargo pants. Those pockets filled up, leaving me to fill the pockets by my knees. Those became stuffed. I had two small, shallow pockets on my hoodie. Each could only hold about five pieces without slipping out. Those were packed within minutes. My last resort was my hood. As my hands became full while walking back towards the house, I resorted to using my hood, not caring about the stares I received from others combing the sand bar and freeing up my hands to find more sea glass when I thought we were done.

We were far from done. My hood ended up holding four handfuls. By the time I stepped off the sand bar, my hands were clutching dozens of pieces.

Uncle Bill and Susan were relaxing on the lawn reading *The New York Post* and *The New York Times*. I was surprised to see them out sunning so early.

"You've been gone a while," Uncle Bill noted. "Did you walk all the way out?"

"No," I replied, realizing I didn't know how long I was gone. "What time is it?" I asked, assuming it was probably mid-morning.

Susan picked up her cell phone. "It's about 12:30 pm."

I couldn't believe how late it was.

"Wait 'til you see what I found." I showed them what was in my hands.

"Oh cool . . . sea glass," Uncle Bill noted.

Susan looked up from the newspaper. "The recycling bin is next to the door in the garage."

"No, Susan," Uncle Bill explained, "I don't think she was picking up trash to recycle."

So far from trash—rather the pieces of sea glass were pieces of a conversation I never thought I'd ever experience. "Susan, check out how much I found!" I exclaimed, wanting to tell the story of how this happened.

"Wow, you really found a lot!" Uncle Bill said.

I knew they wouldn't think I was nuts if I told them about the experience. "Wanna know how I found it all?"

"Sure," Susan replied.

I took a deep breath. "Honestly, at the start of my walk, in my mind I asked my dad to help me find sea glass. It worked."

They didn't ask me what I meant, and from the looks on their faces I didn't know if they completely understood, but it was hard to ignore the over one hundred pieces of sea glass.

CHAPTER 8

Butterflies

IT NEVER OCCURRED TO ME that my mom would remarry. Seven years after my dad passed, we had established a strong pattern of living together. We both worked, came home, ate dinner together, and watched TV. Repeat. Some nights I went out with friends. Some nights she went out. But most nights were that same stagnant pattern: come home after work, eat dinner, watch TV.

Coming home late one Thursday night after being out with friends, I noticed my mom wasn't home yet. I hadn't remembered her saying she was going out to dinner with her girlfriends, but I assumed that's where she was. After changing into my pajamas and brushing my teeth, I heard my mom walk up the stairs. "Oh, hi!" she said, noticing I was just about ready for bed. "Where did you go tonight?"

"I was out with friends for dinner," I yawned, feeling tired. "I got in a little bit ago. Where were you?"

I wasn't expecting her to look directly into my eyes with the intent to tell me something I never expected. "I went out on a date with a guy I met on Match.com."

I was now wide awake. "Really? You went on a date tonight with someone you met online?"

"Yeah," she said with a smirk.

What had become familiar, that cozy pattern of getting ready in the morning, going to work, coming home, and having dinner together and ending our day watching the same TV shows every night, showed its first sign of breaking. "So what's he like?" I found myself asking, surprised at my genuine interest in this guy while thoughts of my dad reappeared. It had been a while since I thought of him.

"He's a pharmaceutical salesman."

I didn't know what to say, so I said nothing.

"And I'm seeing him again in a few days."

We ended the conversation by saying goodnight. I went to bed thinking of my dad, wondering what he'd think while sorting what I felt. What ultimately surfaced was a reminder that my dad was not here. I was sad for days, hoping my mom wouldn't notice so as not to hold her back from happiness.

She did see the salesman a few days later. They went out on a daytime date, which was their last date after the daylight revealed he had probably lied about his age on his profile. Not long after that, she met Vince, a retired chemical engineer and widower with three grown children, all married, and three grandchildren. He was the same age as my mom.

Mom was quickly swept off her feet. She saw Vince nearly every day after their first date. It seemed like she paid more attention to how she styled her hair and what jewelry she wore. Her face had more color, like a light of excitement had returned to her. She wasn't home as much for dinner, our pattern breaking further. Less than two years later, it was their wedding day, solidifying a new way of life for both of us.

Mom's relationship with Vince was entirely different from what my mom had with my dad. It was cute watching them complete *The New York Times* crossword puzzle together, debating over whose answer was correct. My parents never did that. They enjoyed violin concerts and lectures nearly every week. My parents never did that. Even how they looked at each other was different—not better, not worse, just different. My mom read Vince's first wife's books. Photos of my dad remained on display. It was clear that neither was a replacement for a deceased spouse, rather a door opening to a new chapter in life.

Still, the morning of her wedding, thoughts of my dad popped up at every moment. I couldn't ignore it. While I gathered things I needed to take over to Vince's townhouse to get ready, the thoughts distracted me. Worried I'd forget something, I stopped rushing around and took a moment to entertain the thoughts. I wondered most particularly how he would feel about my mom remarrying. I sat down, hoping stillness would bring me some insight. Instead, I felt foggy. Now running out of time, I got up and moved at a slightly more frantic pace. I checked my bags dozens of times, making sure I wasn't forgetting anything while thoughts of my dad continued to distract me. I double checked and triple checked that I had my makeup bag, my hair dryer, my styling products and brushes, my dress, my undergarments, my jewelry, my shoes, my handbag, my cell phone, my camera, the guest book, and my house key, and then I headed for the door. I slammed the door unintentionally hard, jammed my key into the lock, and turned it until I heard the click of the bolt, perhaps my subconscious way of barricading those thoughts of my dad inside the house. I wanted him to stay home so I could focus on the wedding.

It turns out I didn't need my subconscious protecting me. It turns out I didn't need to debate my dad's happiness at all. Just like when I found sea glass on that sand bar in Connecticut, I felt a whisper just as I stepped off the porch. It told me to look up to my left. Gazing up to the bright, hazy morning sky, the biggest, most brilliant monarch butterfly I had ever seen appeared. It was bigger than biggest—the size of a salad plate. Its orange-yellow hues glowed against its black outlined wings. More than eye-catching, it grabbed my soul and captured all of my attention. It flew right toward me, wings fluttering with excitement, as if it was showing off its boldness and grandness. It came within inches of my face and then quickly climbed upward to my right, meeting the tops of the trees and leaving my sight. With that, the question I had carried all morning was answered. *He's completely okay with today.*

The rest of the day felt Zen-like. At the reception, I pulled my mom aside and told her what I had seen, to which she replied her friend often felt her loved ones who had passed came to her as butterflies. It was years later that I realized how much more profound that moment was. My dad was a large man. He was the *monarch* of our immediate family as well as our extended family, and perhaps to some, a monarch of our community. He was often described as a gentle giant, a presence in a room, one of strength and peace simultaneously, perhaps just like an unusually large butterfly.

Then even more years later, I remembered that last drive and *Butterfly Kisses*.

DURING A DAY OFF from work on a perfect June day, I took a day trip down to Island Beach State Park, the southern tip of a barrier island just north of Long

Beach Island where my family used to vacation. Having spent several long days at my office, my goal was to relax on a beach chair by myself on the water's edge, the east wind off the ocean keeping me comfortable on a hot summer day. Sunscreen, snacks, and water. I was prepared to stay there from morning until sunset, soaking up as much serenity as possible. Just as I sat down, I noticed two sailboats and a barge far off the coast. As I watched them slowly move south on the horizon, a butterfly passed by, dancing in the ocean breeze. One of my dad's favorite things was watching the water and noticing everything—boats, swimmers, dolphins, seagulls. From the deck of the second-floor duplex we rented in Surf City, which overlooked the beach, I watched him sit in his beach chair, looking out at the water. He was often the last one to head back to the house.

Since then, nearly every trip to I take to Island Beach State Park, I see a butterfly.

Ten years after my dad passed, I went to Japan to travel and study acupuncture with a group of other practitioners. A trip of a lifetime. We started in Tokyo. On our first day, walking down the street and stopping into various stores, I admired the fabric of a tattered kimono patterned with monarchs. On a day trip to Kamakura, I visited two temples before walking up the hill to see the amazing monumental statue of Amida Buddha, a large bronze statue that in the fifteenth-century survived a tsunami that destroyed the temple surrounding it. Several butterflies fluttered by as I contemplated the missing structure that once protected this great Buddha, thinking it was better off without it, that it was strong enough to stand alone as it gazed out overlooking the Sagami Bay, proudly sitting in its lotus position as it had when its protection washed away.

While walking through the streets of Kyoto, a fan with a butterfly caught my eye as did many other Japanese treasures. Nara was by far the most fun, with thousands of deer roaming freely in front of Tōdai-ji, a Shinto temple. I bought large crackers to feed them and before I knew it I was surrounded by nearly a dozen eager deer all waiting for a bite. After feeding them, we walked toward the temple and entered through its massive doors, where we were greeted by Diabutsu, the world's largest wooden statue of the Buddha Viarocana. At the base of the Buddha was a large metal butterfly. During an unforgettable three-day retreat to Mount Koya, a Buddhist mountain community with over a hundred temples, butterflies appeared on murals and screens while on a historical tour. Even our guide's stitched handbag had a beautiful, large monarch sewn on it.

It was as if my dad had wanted to go on the trip with me.

I opened my acupuncture practice in May 2007. For the first several years, nearly every morning while walking to work, a monarch crossed my path. Some walks to work were preoccupied by thoughts of a busy day or challenging case, and a butterfly greeted me on those mornings, lightening my mood and uplifting my spirit.

To this day, whenever I'm sorting out a problem I notice a butterfly. Whenever I'm having a lot of fun, I notice a butterfly. Even while watching a baseball game at Yankee Stadium, a monarch has appeared.

Hurricane Irene

I ANTICIPATED HURRICANE IRENE throwing me backward. Winds, rain, trees . . . *a thousand cardboard boxes*. I imagined a nightmare ahead. I didn't know what to do to get ready for it other than to pretend everything was normal. I did the usual tasks I do when taking a day off—cleaning, cooking, laundry—followed by reading and watching TV. Luckily for me, I didn't have to try so hard. It ended up being like any other day for me, except there was no way for me to know that ahead of time given the dramatic warnings from the meteorologists.

My fiancé, Mike, and I had bought a house eight months before, feeling excited now to occupy a spot on the planet where we could set down roots. This was the first major storm we'd experience in our new house, a nineteenth-century salt box colonial that had great bones but was a major fixer upper. The house was filled with character, featuring original woodwork and hardwood floors, as well decades of wear and tear. The wear and tear was fixable, but we were only at the beginning. Having always lived in older homes and buildings, I find comfort in knowing they've survived many storms in their lifetimes. The schoolhouse in Syracuse was untouched from that crazy Labor Day weekend storm. Even the 1830's farm house I grew up in wasn't fazed by *a thousand cardboard boxes*. Looking at our fixer upper, I wondered what it had faced.

The storm came in softly, despite the appearance on the radar. Images of high winds and downpours flashed on TV as reporters anchored their stances and shouted through the wind. I looked out the windows from time to time, not wanting to see, but curious if whatever I did see would get to me. The trees swayed, but not dramatically—not like on TV. The rain fell, but no differently than it did during any other summer storm. There were no sounds of *cardboard boxes* . . . not a single one that I could hear. For me, it could have been any other rainy day, but it was labeled a *hurricane.*

That label gave me strength, made me feel triumphant. I'd run from opportunity in Florida because of storms. I still avoided meeting up with friends if a thunderstorm was predicted, even canceling last minute with excuses of not feeling well, which wasn't far from the truth. Unexpectedly, Hurricane Irene did not throw me backward. If anything, I felt propelled forward, ready to let go of my fears.

As the hours passed, I looked outside more often, feeling braver and braver with every glance. Nature looked like it was dancing, grooving to the music of the wind, which appeared more like a swift breeze than a force. I remembered leaving the front podium at the character buffet at Disney when the rain started, retreating to the bathroom, the one room in the center of the building, a room that was safe and didn't appear strange to others why I had to go, other than them thinking I "had to go." I couldn't look then, and I couldn't look that morning, but I was looking now . . . and I really liked what I saw.

"I'm going to step outside and take a look around," Mike said casually.

I hit the jackpot with Mike. Taking a cue from my mom, I went online. We met on OKCupid.com. We talked on the phone for about a month before our first date. We planned on meeting outside Cafe Metro, a quaint restaurant in Denville that happens to be next door to the building that used to house my dad's law practice. When I saw him walking around the corner with a big smile on his face, I knew he would be special to me. After dinner, we walked all over the downtown area. After we'd walked along every street there, we drove to the Boulevard in Mountain Lakes and walked to Island Beach. We watched swans gliding along the surface of the calm water as the sun set. It was a date I didn't want to end, but we did end it after we left the beach.

A few days later, we went on a long, strenuous hike by the Delaware Water Gap. Even though we were sweaty and disgusting after our four-hour hike, we stopped at a diner for a midafternoon meal. We drove a scenic way home, passing by various important places we both liked, including the house where I grew up. Beyond extending the date for a second time, it was a way of showing each other snippets of our lives. I later learned Mike loved helping people, that he loved cars and owned a '68 Corvette with his father, and that even though he struggled in school he was highly intelligent when it came to mechanical thinking and despite his high school guidance counselor telling him he'd never make it through technical school, he completed it and landed an information technology job right away.

Mike's other gifts included being generous with his time, checking in and being there for his friends, acting with integrity, and always doing his best to choose right over wrong. His face always held a smile even when he didn't feel well.

Eventually I told Mike what happened. It was the first time I saw his smile lessen as he heard about *a thousand cardboard boxes*. He didn't know what to say, but I reassured him that I was okay, even though thoughts of hurricanes and storms made me wonder if I was indeed okay. He liked fixing things, making them better, and our colonial was a labor of love for him. I wasn't going to stop him from going outside to check on things, even though the hurricane wasn't over and I knew how storms could change in an instant.

Instead, I found myself saying something I didn't expect. "I'll join you."

Mike's bright blue eyes grew wide as they often do on his face that never lies. "Really? Are you sure?"

"Yes. I'm fine," I reassured, albeit uncertainly, as I put my bright blue pashmina around my neck.

Mike unlocked the French door and stepped outside, surveying the yard and the perimeter of the house. I followed, stepping onto the gravel patio, staying near the door. My legs felt like Jell-O. Cautious, slightly shaking, feeling my heart race just a little. Taking it in. The trees weren't dancing as much. The overcast sky moved with blotchy dark and white clouds, slowly swirling in different directions. As much as I worried I'd see destruction if I looked, now I saw calm within the storm. I carefully walked into our back yard and met Mike as he walked back from the sheds.

"The sheds are fine," he mentioned as me passed me, continuing on with his inspection.

I stayed put in the middle of the yard, telling myself this was over. *No more PTSD. No more haunting thoughts. I can look. I can stand within it. I am done. Cured.*

No longer afflicted. It's gone, I told myself. *I have over-come.* For the first time since *a thousand cardboard boxes,* I felt completely free. I slowly turned around, watching the trees, taking each one in, admiring their different movements. Some swayed. Some fluttered. Some leaned. The sky continued its gray patchy transformation. I wondered how strong the winds were above. The air smelled like earth. Cool but comforting. I strolled around the yard, looking down into the pond at the goldfish as I headed towards the vegetable garden that needed to be winterized. Our spot on earth felt more like ours than ever. As I walked towards the side door, l scanned the yard again, grateful to call this place home.

THE NEXT MORNING, Mike left for work. Even though Hurricane Irene had flooded many areas and caused a lot of destruction, he couldn't justify staying home where everything stood perfectly high and dry. In preparation for the worst, before the storm I had already cancelled my patients for the day. I had busied myself with cleaning, cooking, and laundry the morning before as a way to ignore what was happening outside even though it turned out I didn't need to do so. There was nothing to do but the one chore that I'd hated as a child: picking up sticks.

I looked out the back kitchen window and saw many sticks strewn all over the yard. Since Mike enjoyed yard work and I loved to cook, we had an unspoken deal that regarding chores around the house in general he was in charge of the outside and I was in charge of the inside. Still, knowing he was at work and I had the day off, I couldn't leave this for him to do. I put on my sweats and sneakers, went down to the basement to get a bucket, and stepped outside through the garage. I looked at our acre of open space that was dotted by numerous trees, thinking about the best way to start, and headed toward the side yard. Less than a minute into picking them up, I realized I needed a much bigger bucket.

If my dad was looking down on me at that moment, he was probably laughing. Gayle and I hate yard work, something our dad made us do nearly every weekend. He would start by asking us if we could "give him a hand." As kids, we never said no, since it was dad asking us to do something. It wasn't until I was a teenager that I wondered what the consequence would be if I said no. So one weekend morning after I noticed my dad wearing his yard work jeans and white tee-shirt with holes, I hid upstairs in my room pretending to be busy, waiting for my dad's weekly question.

"Hey Sue?" my dad called up the stairs to me.

"What?"

"Can you give me a hand?"

"No."

Silence. I waited to see what would happen, but nothing did. I couldn't see his reaction, imagining him thinking of a response to my *no*, hoping he wasn't angry with me. I waited quietly in my room until I could hear him move away from the steps. A few minutes later, I glanced out my bedroom window that overlooked the back yard and saw my dad picking up sticks. A tiny part of me felt bad knowing he was doing this by himself even though I hated doing it. Still, I relaxed in my bed with a book and celebrated my freedom from yard work.

A half hour later . . .

"Hey Sue?" my dad called.

"What?"

"Give me a hand."

He wasn't harsh or angry or stern, but he was no longer asking me.

"Alright," I replied.

I changed into my yard work clothes and headed outside to meet my dad. Yard work was the worst. Gayle and I were very fortunate to have a wonderfully large back yard to play in when we were growing up, but having a large yard meant picking up a lot of sticks and raking a lot of leaves. My dad would often say he just needed us for a half hour, as if he was a little guilty for needing his own kids help in maintaining such a big space instead of doing something fun together. A half hour usually meant two hours, and more often than not, after two hours we were only halfway finished with what needed to be done. Sometimes we did yard work the whole day all the way up to dinnertime. Gayle and I hated it. I hated bending down over and over again picking up sticks, leaves, chestnuts, and whatever else the trees decided to drop. Yard work would then sometimes evolve into sweeping the garage and front porch. Then it would evolve again into sweeping the gravel at the end of the driveway. It was tiring and boring for hours and hours. The light at the end of the yard work tunnel was usually pizza, which always tasted better on those nights than others.

Twenty years later, Mike and I were now responsible for our own house and our own yard. I went back into the garage and found a bigger bucket, which was actually the garbage can. Returning to the side yard, I got to work. I lost count after twelve garbage cans. I worked up a sweat and sore calves walking up and down the hill dumping each bucket behind the sheds. I thought about those Saturday afternoons with my dad doing yard work. I saw him sitting on the tractor cutting grass while I picked up sticks behind the swing set. I remembered him raking leaves into a pile for me to pick up and put into a bucket. As I got older, that system evolved into raking leaves onto a big blue tarp that we then picked up at the corners to dump in the woods.

I thought about the dust getting stirred in the garage as we swept, the chestnuts plopping into the bucket as we tossed them in, piling chopped wood into the trailer to bring up to the porch to then stack into the wood ring . . . usually the only time my dad allowed me to drive the tractor myself.

As these memories came back with each load of sticks I gathered, it hit me that even though I hated yard work, these moments made me smile. For my dad, it wasn't only about having a beautifully manicured, lush green lawn with no weeds and perfect mow lines, and it wasn't only about instilling in me and Gayle that to have such a nice lawn required a lot of work. I finally got it that ultimately it was about him spending time with us, even if it meant doing something none of us really wanted to do.

It took me an hour and a half to pick up the sticks in our yard. It was the first time I ever enjoyed it.

WHILE MEMORIES FLOODED my mind, the news showed house after house flooded by water in nearby areas. Helicopters flew over house fires that burned out of control because water surrounding entire neighborhoods kept firetrucks away. Each house looked like island infernos in the middle of water, even more heartbreaking to watch knowing that the solution to putting out the fire was everywhere but where it needed to be. Displaced people told their stories of losing everything and having nowhere to go. Their stories struck me. As this storm turned things around for me, it turned things upside-down for others.

I thought about Denville and how downtown used to flood enough to cause inconvenience due to road closures and people pumping out their basements. But it was never worse than that. It wasn't until I saw a video posted by a friend on Facebook showing a person riding a jet ski on Broadway, right in the middle of town, that I knew this was different. The water from a storm normally was never that deep. Between downtown and the Rockaway River was a neighborhood of numerous homes. I began to imagine their nightmares.

The imaginings became real as I read stories in the local news. The water came so fast that people didn't have a change to escape. Instead, they climbed to the highest points in their home while water rushed through broken windows, swirling mud and debris among their belongings. One story described the water rising up so fast that it trapped their cat in the basement, and the only way to free their beloved pet was to cut a hole in their floor to rescue it just in time. There was no time to grab heirlooms or documents, just barely enough to grab each other to scramble to find safety. I pictured frantic shouts, children crying, dogs barking, and whatever sounds that came from rushing water. That sound, whatever it sounded like . . . I wondered . . . was that their *thousand cardboard boxes?*

Donations poured in. I purchased ten $10 gift cards from the local supermarket and gave them to town hall, a stone's throw away from the devastation. It didn't feel like enough. Roads leading in were blocked off by police, allowing only homeowners and cleaning crews access. Rumors spread of businesses closing. I thought about Denville Dairy, a place I'd gone to hundreds of times for ice cream, its popularity required taking a number to be served and sometimes waiting nearly an hour before being called. Faith and Begora, an Irish store owned by the mother of a childhood friend, stood on the corner of Broadway and First Avenue, right in the heart of town, at one of the lowest elevations. Grassroots Natural Market, a place I frequented for lunch, was perched on a decent number of stairs, giving me hope that they were spared. Urban Muse, my favorite spa, sat right next to the river. I thought about all of these businesses and others.

I later learned that all of these places were damaged. The damage totaled over six-figures for one business alone.

Loss of stuff... of income... of livelihood... What I couldn't ignore were the thoughts of what might be lingering under the pressing issues of the moment ...loss of peace.

I had to do something. A few years before, I took a continuing education course on helping people affected by natural disasters using acupuncture through Acupuncturists Without Borders (AWB), an organization that began in 2005 after Hurricane Katrina devastated the Gulf Coast. Following that hurricane, a group of acupuncturists led by Diana Fried, an acupuncturist from New Mexico, felt compelled to drive to New Orleans after seeing the news footage of people suffering in the Superdome and surrounding areas for days with little or no help. Diana and her team set up a makeshift acupuncture clinic on a street corner, offering free acupuncture treatments for anyone who needed stress relief. It was such a huge success that their efforts went on for months, eventually drawing acupuncturists from all parts of the country to fly in and assist them with treatments. Soon after, they got their nonprofit status and, following other disasters, have since provided over one million treatments for stress relief. They have also trained over 2,500 acupuncturists across the United States and many health care providers internationally. It is considered one of the leading nonprofit organizations within the acupuncture field.

The course I took outlined how one would open and operate a relief clinic following a natural disaster. Besides teaching how to run a clinic, the instructors went into great detail about PTSD, explaining that while not everyone will experience PTSD after a disaster, it's important to understand the needs of people who may eventually develop it: being sensitive, listening, knowing what to do if people get emotional, positioning ourselves to keep people comfortable. Their ultimate goal in teaching these classes was to have trained acupuncture practitioners all over the country who could set up a relief clinic quickly if one was needed. I knew this type of clinic could be my way of helping others deal with the trauma of what happened.

I contacted AWB who then connected me to Toni Groelly, an acupuncturist in Montville, a town right next to where I practice in Boonton. Toni had also taken the AWB training and was already working on starting up a relief clinic. She had paperwork and supplies in place, but was hitting roadblocks in finding a location for the clinic. Typically, AWB suggests contacting churches, fire departments, and other municipal offices for setting up a temporary clinic, especially if there were already relief efforts happening at those locations. Toni tried many of these avenues, but was met with fears about acupuncture and liability concerns.

It turns out that I had a patient who happened to know a lot of Denville business owners, and she was already working on fundraising to help them. After speaking with her, she contacted a gallery owner toward the end of downtown who miraculously did not have any flood damage despite being located right next to the river. Her building was just high enough that everything was safe. The gallery owner allowed us to use her space for a clinic.

After meeting to review the procedures, double checking our supplies, posting flyers around town, and talking to a reporter from *The Daily Record* who published an article about the clinic that very morning, we were ready to go. The unexpected happened only five minutes after opening. As I was putting acupuncture needles into the first patient, someone came in asking for me. I handed off the patient to Toni and stepped away, wondering who was saying hello. I was greeted by a man I didn't know. I'll call him "Kent."

Kent introduced himself. I had never heard his name before, but he knew who I was from reading the article that morning in *The Daily Record*. After the initial pleasantries, he stared at me wide eyed.

"Can I help you?" I asked as a knot developed in my stomach even before I knew what was about to come.

"Are you related to Ron Pitman?"

This was a question I frequently was asked in the years following my dad's passing. Fourteen years later and I was still being asked. I confirmed that I was his daughter, not realizing it would bring a deluge of questions.

"How long ago was the accident?"

"Was it a tree that hit your dad?"

"Wasn't he mowing the lawn when it happened?"

"I thought your mother witnessed it, not you?"

"Was he dead after it happened?"

"How did the tree break apart?"

"Did the whole tree fall over?"

"Was he hit by the actual tree?"

"Did your house get damaged?"

"You lived in that yellow house on the corner with the well, didn't you?"

"What were his injuries?"

"What happened to his law firm?"

"Wasn't Kurt Senesky also in the firm?"

"Do you still live in that house?"

"Where do you live now?"

"How's your mom doing?"

The knot grew bigger and bigger, to the point where my body wanted to shake while I tried to keep my cool. Blindsided, I didn't know how to get out of the verbal assault, which is what it felt like, believing it would end with each question. The only question I had been asked in the last fourteen years was if I was related to Ron Pitman. The confirmation that I was his daughter always satisfied the curiosity, which still stung because sometimes it brought me back to *a thousand cardboard boxes*. I never thought I would be asked these things.

He kept going, leaving me no choice but to explain that I was needed in the clinic and walk away, even though no one else had come in for treatment yet. Toni and Mike watched the whole thing, not knowing what to do, also shocked by this man's gall. After he left, we agreed that anyone who wanted to speak with me needed to be prescreened, something I had never ever thought in a million years would be necessary.

More people came to the clinic. I busied myself providing treatment, making sure people were comfortable, but remained cautious with each encounter. *Did they know?* A few more people came by asking for me, but Mike explained I was busy. After we were done for the night, I asked Mike who stopped by. One of them was the owner of Faith and Begora. I would have loved to have said hello to her. It made me sad that something spoiled that.

As soon as I got home from wrapping up the clinic, I called my mom to ask her who Kent was. She had difficulty placing him, believing he may have been involved with some town projects and my dad possibly knew him peripherally. My mom didn't even know his wife's name. He was definitely not a friend. He wasn't someone who knew us. We weren't even sure he was in the crowd of hundreds who were at the wake or the funeral. We doubted we even received a sympathy card from him.

"I just don't understand why this guy thought those questions were okay," I told my mom. "I mean, didn't he think asking me those things would hurt? Are people really that insensitive?"

"I understand why you're hurt," my mom sympathized, "but I think most people in Denville who were living in town at the time and who heard about it don't see it that way at first. Their first thought is that it was a town tragedy."

Not just ours . . . theirs as well . . . even still to that day I struggled with this.

I brushed it off, remembering that Hurricane Irene had given me bigger gifts. Besides helping others, I had let go of my PTSD. I smiled believing storms would no longer affect my life. I hung onto that feeling so much that I got complacent, having no idea that I would be pulled back into it two months later.

CHAPTER 10

October Snowstorm

SNOW! AS A CHILD, SNOW was nature's magical crystals. At school, it interrupted class the moment someone spotted the first flakes. With just that one shrill of excitement, every kid jumped from their desk and ran towards the window, anticipating covered hills for sledding, building snowmen and forts, and rolling around in its cold, wet, deceptive softness that only comes for a few months of the entire year. Snow meant play, a break from school. Snow was whimsy. Snow meant icicles to lick like popsicles. Everything about snow was fun.

Even as the responsibilities of shoveling, throwing down salt, and clearing my car came with adulthood, to me snow was still magical. Sticking to every limb and stick on trees forming white, spiky sculptures arching over roadways, snow created tunnels of beauty. Red cardinals, the only bright color against the white ground and gray skies, brought vibrancy. The desire to cook hearty meals and snuggle up under the covers with a full belly while the snow floated down to the ground felt nurturing. Sunlit sparkling diamonds across a white blanket. Foxes breaking its smooth surface while leaping through the yard. Ice dripping to form stalactites, all different lengths and shapes, never to form the same shape again as they glowed in the sun. To me, snow was exquisite.

Never ever did I imagine snow would create *a thousand cardboard boxes.*

Even with several warnings from meteorologists of the impending snowstorm, I never thought it would throw me backward. A rare, late October snowstorm was imminent, and all I cared about was cooking butternut squash soup and my first turkey meatloaf. Dozens of times, I heard them say snow would stick to trees and power lines, causing downed limbs and outages. But all I pictured were those tunnels of beauty. Weather maps showed over a foot of wet, heavy snow coming to our area, snow that would stick to trees that still had their brilliant red, yellow, and orange leaves. Every report guaranteed this snowstorm would create a disastrous situation. None of it registered with me. Perhaps it was because of my triumphant feeling after Hurricane Irene just weeks before. Perhaps it was my desire to hold onto the magic of snow from my childhood. Perhaps it was because of my love for cooking and wanting to create the perfect meal for our first major snowstorm in our house. Perhaps it was all of it, combined with never thinking I could come close to living through something unimaginable twice.

Even when the two tall birch trees that sat behind the garden bed behind our house began to gracefully bend over towards our bedroom window, it still seemed like fun as I watched Mike take a chain saw to their bases, saving our window and siding from any significant damage as our cats Penny and Gizmo peered out the window with tremendous wonder, pawing at the sticks that touched the screen, creating a tiny tear. Afterward, he chopped away all of the shrubbery along the fence between our side yard and the road. They were sagging with snow. Rather than forming tunnels of beauty, they created clumpy barriers blocking the road. Coming in drenched with snow and sweat from his work, Mike couldn't believe how heavy it was. Only four inches had fallen, but they were wet and came rapidly, enough so that plows could not keep up. Despite Mike's efforts in keeping the road cleared from the collapsed brush, a plow never passed by . . . not even after the snow stopped falling.

I spent the early part of the afternoon snuggled on the couch reading *Better Homes and Gardens* while the TV repeated the weather report in the background. While folding down corners of ideas for home improvements and recipes, I heard alarming phrases— *historic snow event . . . once in a lifetime . . . trees will fall . . . there will be widespread power outages*—but those words still did nothing to me. I was lost in the whimsy of what snow was supposed to be, sometimes stopping to think about dinner, looking forward to those warm, savory flavors. Occasionally, I glanced up out the window to marvel at the white blankets forming. Our road was quiet.

I went to the kitchen to start dinner. I started with an onion, chopping it up and sliding it off the wooden cutting board and into the thick pot already warming with olive oil. The sizzling sounds only enhanced the peace I felt as I moved onto the butternut squash, slicing off the skin, its bright orange flesh seeping out dew that stuck to every crevice of my hands. As much as I loved cooking butternut squash, no matter how many times I'd wash my hands, they would still feel sticky the next day. But I could not have cared less as I cut it up into inch-sized cubes and added it to the pot as the room filled with more aromas.

I moved on to the turkey meatloaf, opting not to follow a recipe, but rather just to wing it. More onion chopped along with carrots. I added them to a bowl of ground turkey, breadcrumbs, tomato paste, herbs, and an egg, squeezing and smashing it together until turning into a grayish-pink blob. Without a mold, I formed two loaves on a cookie sheet and placed them in the oven.

Mike came in, having stepped outside to snow blow a third time in only five hours. "I can't believe how much snow we have already! It's unbelievable! By the way, your cooking smells awesome outside," he mentioned as he pointed to the range hood that sucked out the smoke from the caramelizing vegetables as I added the chicken stock, steam violently rising from the pot.

The snow did look unbelievable. The bright autumn leaves were now masked by a thick coating, causing limbs to droop. Shrubbery now flattened from the weight. A large lilac bush was now an unrecognizable white mound. It looked otherworldly. Snow never looked like a heavy down comforter before. Despite losing the birch trees, the bushes along the road and the continuous warnings by reporters blaring from the TV, the beauty still captivated me. In between stirring the pot, I watched it fall outside the French doors. The comforter looked cozy, perhaps protective.

After blending the soup, setting the table, and calling for Mike, who was hungry from hours of clearing wet snow, I opened the fridge to grab a chilled bottle of chardonnay.

CLICK.

No warning. No flickering. One loud click and we were in the dark. The only light left came from the deep overcast sky, which was fading fast. I quickly shut the fridge, instinctually protecting its contents, but forgetting to grab the wine. I didn't want to open it again, even though I knew the wine would make the meal even more enjoyable than I already foretasted. In hindsight, I should have opened the fridge.

"That didn't sound good," Mike noted as he walked toward the window at the front of the house, checking the power lines and neighbor's houses.

It was obvious we lost power, but I didn't get Mike's concern. "Why do you say that?"

"Well," he explained, "that click didn't sound good. The power didn't fade out like a brown out. Something major must have happened somewhere in the grid."

I grew concerned. "But our house is okay?"

"Yeah, we're okay. Maybe it's a substation or something. The whole neighborhood is probably out." Mike looked at the oven. "How much longer did that have?"

My first turkey meatloaf still had about ten minutes to go. "Not that much longer. I'll leave it in there another twenty minutes and let the remaining heat in the oven cook it. I'd rather it be dry than not done." My concern washed away after Mike reassured me the house was fine. I walked toward the dry sink, opened the drawer, and pulled out two white tapered candles to put into the pewter chambersticks. The cozy meal I had planned now had candlelight, an element I hadn't thought of adding. Even without power, the day felt enhanced.

We ate our butternut squash soup at our kitchen table, the candles bringing a soft glow that transported me to what I believed the first dinners in our house were like. With the outage came silence. Gone were the hums and buzzes from all of the appliances, the trickling sound of the water in the baseboard heaters. I'd never heard such quiet in our house before. Only our discussions and the spoons clinking against the ceramic bowls broke the silence.

"We'll need to keep warm tonight," Mike warned. "Temperatures are going to drop with all of this snow and by the sound of that click we might be out for a while."

"How long do you think?" I asked, thinking more about the wonderful taste of the soup than the impending problems ahead.

"Not sure," Mike replied. "At least a day. Probably more. After dinner we should put on more layers just in case."

I cleared our soup bowls and brought them to the sink. Only then did I remember we had well water, realizing I could not rinse them as I reached toward the faucet. "So this means we have no water, right?" I asked, noticing I still had the sticky residue of the butternut squash on my hands despite having washed them several times.

"Yup."

The consequences of that click began to sink in. "So obviously we can't shower, but we can't flush the toilet either."

"Yup, so no flushing for tonight. Probably shouldn't put paper in the bowl."

I pulled the turkey meatloaf from the warm oven. "Oh well, I guess there are worse things," I rationalized as I sliced into the loaf, checking in the dim light from my cell phone to see that it was done. I plated two large slices for each of us and brought them to the table.

"At least we'll have just had a warm meal," Mike said as he took his first bite. "*Mmm!* This turned out good!"

I looked at my plate and the rest of the meatloaf on the cookie sheet. "I'm glad. Too bad we can't put it in the fridge after we eat it."

"We can put it in Tupperware and stick it in the garage. It's a constant forty degrees in there right now. It'll be fine." Eating dinner warmed my belly, returned that cozy feeling I imagined many had enjoyed in our house back in the nineteenth century. I soaked in the silence, the candlelight, the stillness that settled into our home, wishing our hectic lives today had that same stillness. That click created something nice.

"Imagine the first people who lived in this house, who probably ate meals in the dark like we are now." I fantasized to Mike. "It's kind of nice."

Mike thought about it. "Yeah, it is kind of nice. It's really quiet now."

"I know. I just love that right now."

After finishing our meatloaf, we wrapped the leftovers in aluminum foil and placed them in large zip bags. Mike carried them down to the garage with a flashlight while I placed the unrinsed plates in the dishwasher along with our soup bowls and utensils. I settled back onto the couch under the hand knit patchwork blanket made by my great-grandmother, picturing her and her family using it on cold winter days in their frontier home. The silence. The darkness. The candlelight. The only entertainment was the beauty of outside and conversation between me and Mike. *This is what life was like during simpler times.* Safe inside while the cold thickened outside. I thought about Laura Ingalls Wilder's memoir *The Long Winter* and how her family sat together around a fire for days at a time, conserving their energy. Their only task was to keep warm and ration their food— not an easy time. Still, I wondered if they found a similar peace.

Mike returned from the garage. "*Brrrr!* It sure is cold outside!"

I looked out the window, noticing the sky turning a deeper blue as night fell. "How much do you think we got?"

"At least a foot and it's still falling."

I grabbed my phone and clicked on my weather app. The radar showed heavy bands in the area. The winter weather watch predicted up to fourteen inches. "I don't think we're done," I mentioned as I clicked on Facebook, wondering what my friends were saying about the snow. It surprised me that only a small handful of them were also sharing stories and pictures of their totals.

"To save battery life, you should probably not use your phone," Mike cautioned, "since you can't charge it."

I shut it off, wondering what I was going to do to occupy myself while waiting for the power to return. I picked up *Martha Stewart Living*, flipped through pages and turned down corners. The remaining outside light coming in from the window provided enough for me to see. We sat in silence for several minutes. During that time, my mind quieted. I pictured myself sitting around the fire with the Ingalls family, imagining the crackling and flashing flames filling the household with warmth as the wind howled outside. We had it better. There were no winds. We each had our own closets overflowing with clothes to keep us warm. Somehow, we had accumulated over a dozen blankets between the two of us. Our fridge and freezer were well stocked after having shopped for food that morning.

I'd never lived without power for more than a day, so I imagined taking the meatloaf from the garage and putting it in the fridge the next day, using the oven to reheat it. Our cell phones still worked. Life barely interrupted. There was nothing to worry about and perhaps everything to enjoy. Right now, we didn't have to go to work. Right now, we didn't need to pay bills. Right now, all of life's stressors were put on the back burner, all thanks to that *click*. No internet. No emails. No distractions. Now was really nice. Now was peaceful. Now was to be enjoyed before it went away.

My enjoyment was much shorter than I expected.

Breaking the silence was that all too familiar sound I've only ever heard once. *Rip.* It didn't stop there, growing to more and more *rips*. I looked up from my magazine to see a wide-eyed Mike looking back at me. It was coming from the southeast side of the house. It kept growing, crescendoing from *a thousand cardboard boxes* to TEN *thousand cardboard boxes*. I leapt from the couch and moved toward the middle of the house. *BOOM!* The sound shook the entire house, rattling the windows and causing every glass, every candle holder, and every knickknack to quiver. It moved through the house to the other side. *RIP.* A different kind of noise, but still sounding like wood, coming from the northwest corner. *RIP. Rip. Rip* . . . silence.

Mike jumped up from the recliner and ran to the front window. "Holy shit!"

I knew what it was. An image of my dad flashed in my mind. "Did it hit the house?"

Mike raced from window to window, examining the situation from all angles. "HOLY SHIT!"

"DID IT HIT THE HOUSE?" More images flashed: *rain, wind, emergency lights, the stretcher.*

"No, but look at all the wires!"

I looked out the window, the same one that only moments ago had been providing me with the last bit of daylight. Several power and cable lines jiggled and swayed. Looking down toward the garage, I saw a tangle of wires. "What's all that?" I asked Mike.

He came and stood behind me, looking out the window. "Holy shit! It must have pulled all the wires from the house."

Yes . . . *it.* I knew, but didn't want to know. I wanted the flashing to stop.

"Come look out this window," Mike motioned to me as he led me toward the dining room.

My fears of what it was were true. It was a tree, the tree on the border of our property and our next-door neighbor's. The one that had looked precarious when I walked the property with the home inspector. It was bigger, louder. It was also hollow. It broke in half, blocking the entire road. As it ripped apart, it fell into all nine utility lines, bringing them to the ground while tearing the connection off the side of our house, snapping a telephone pole in half and splintering another one further down the street. The only thing it didn't do was fall on someone, but that didn't stop my mind from feeling like it did. Panic set in and my heart raced. It didn't matter that we were okay, that our house wasn't hit. I wanted to run away. I worried that because of this heavy, white down comforter covering everything outside that more *cardboard boxes* could happen.

I grabbed my phone to call Julia, one of my closest friends. Hours earlier, we talked on the phone about the snow. She was only twenty minutes away and barely had any.

"Who are you calling?" Mike asked.

"Julia. Because we have to get out of here."

Mike didn't hesitate with his response. "I don't think that's a good idea."

His suggestion meant nothing to me. "We can't stay here. She and Mart will come get us."

"I don't think they'll be able to get here. The roads are probably closed."

"They have the Explorer. They drive in any snow."

"They won't be able to get to the house."

"We'll wear layers and walk to Route 10 if we have to."

"Susannah," Mike's alarm growing. "It's not a good idea!"

"WE CAN'T STAY HERE! WE HAVE TO GET AWAY FROM THIS!"

Even though years ago I told Mike the story, I realized he wasn't getting it. Frustration that he wasn't agreeing to my plan built as I feverishly tapped my phone searching for Julia's number. I hit it hard once I found it, speaking a mile a minute and asking her to come pick us up. Minutes later, she called back saying the highway was closed and she couldn't make it. It sunk in deep that I couldn't leave, that Mike didn't understand, and that this could happen again at any time.

"I knew they couldn't come," Mike couldn't help saying.

I wanted to smack him. Instead, I took a deep breath, fighting an urge to scream at the man I loved. "You don't understand. This is bringing me back to my dad's accident. If that tree fell, more could fall. I can't go through this again!"

Mike's posture changed. He stopped moving from window to window, assessing the damage. He walked up to me and put his arms around my shoulders as I stared out the window at the dead tree.

"We'll be okay," he reassured as he let go and walked toward the basement door. "I'm going to the garage to see how bad it is." He quickly opened and closed the door behind him with flashlight in hand. I could hear him climbing down the wooden steps and opening the door into the garage. For the first time, the house felt cold as if the life was sucked from it. I looked toward the steps, feeling scared to go upstairs, which was the same feeling I had fourteen years earlier. I saw flashes of rocking, staring out my bedroom window at the tree tops, and Aunt Barbara watching me sleep on the couch. Every detail flooded back. I wanted to stop them. I walked toward the stairs and looked up them, searching for courage not to go backward. I took the first step, the second one, still shaking. By the time I got to the top, I found myself using my hands to help me crawl up the stairs. Penny and Gizmo ran from room to room, crouched down with poufy backs and tails, clearly knowing something had happened.

"It's alright," I told Penny as I reached for her, remembering Mickey in the crawl space in the basement. Mickey later resting his cheek on my dad's shoes . . . more flashes.

I grabbed silk long underwear, yoga pants, lined nylon pants, a long sleeve tee-shirt, a sweat shirt, and a knitted hat from my closet and started layering up. Mike came into the bedroom as I was putting on my hat. "You said we should put on layers," I reminded him.

He started to root through his closet looking for the warmest clothes. I walked toward the bedroom window, looking at everything drooping, sagging. One tree in the middle of our back yard appeared precarious.

"The kitties are spooked," I told Mike. "We should probably let them sleep with us tonight, you know, in case something happens so we don't have to look for them."

Normally, this is a big request. Penny, an older gray and white tuxedo, preferred sleeping on top of one of us so that it's difficult to turn over and get comfortable. Gizmo, a cat just out of kittenhood with black and white patchy fur, never stayed still for longer than ten minutes. He preferred running on the bed, chasing whatever foot or hand that moved, jumping up on the dresser and knocking things over to do whatever possible to keep us awake.

"Yeah, they can sleep with us," Mike replied without hesitation.

Not long after we bundled up, the four of us got in bed. As the skies faded to black, the silence broke with snaps and rips. *Cardboard boxes* in the distance, some closer than I wanted. Each one caused me to shake. Mike spooned me the entire night, holding me tighter each time I trembled. I wanted to rock, but his arms prevented me. Flashes continued, mostly around my dad. I missed him. I hadn't thought about him in a while. Now, images of him—at the beach, swinging a golf club, having dinner, smiling—flashing. *Why is he gone?* I wondered and wished he were not. Thoughts occasionally interrupted by emergency lights, rain, wind, thunder. A few times, *a thousand cardboard boxes*. Each time I forced myself to think about the beach just like I had fourteen years earlier. Penny and Gizmo stayed still, snuggling up by our feet. I imagined they were grateful they could be near us.

Therapy

AS I PULLED INTO THE PARKING LOT of the professional building that blended in with every other professional building along Route 46 in Parsippany, I noticed the day was too nice to be here. It was a sunny and warm November day, one of the last opportunities for such a day that year. As I stepped out of my car and walked the short distance to the door, I wondered if taking a long walk on the Boulevard would be more valuable. Still, I went inside and looked on the directory for Lucille Jengo, LCSW, LMFT, BCD. Those letters behind her name felt heavy. This felt harder than I wanted it to be.

The waiting room was large, the walls lined with the same kind of waiting room chairs that were in all the other professional buildings. Stacks of magazines with the corners curled sat piled in various places. I sat near a children's play table with toys strewn across. Doors lined along a wall like *Let's Make a Deal*. I wondered what was behind, knowing I'd see one of them. I was the only one waiting, which thankfully meant I didn't need to avoid casual, but curious, eye contact with others.

Next to me on a chair were *Newsweek* and *Travel + Leisure*. I picked up *Travel + Leisure* and flipped through the glossy images of perfect, exotic getaways that appeared so far from my reach yet so inviting, like all I had to do was max out my credit card and go, which sounded tempting as I sat in that waiting room chair. Eventually, the lean muscular bodies glowing and laughing on the beach with not a care in the world seemed depressing, so I closed the magazine and put it on top of *Newsweek*, covering up Herman Cain's face and thumbs-up pose with "The Unlikely Rise of the Anti-Obama" under his hand.

I chose not to pull out my phone, figuring that getting lost in a mindless game might catch me off guard when my name eventually was called. I also didn't want to be seen as one of those people who have to be on their phones all the time, even though I was on my phone a lot.

I looked around the room, searching for the most interesting things to capture my attention. The kids' table won. It looked a lot like the play table at the pediatrician's office that I went to as a kid. Same kinds of toys. Same short chairs. I thought about that office, never remembering it as a scary place or a place I didn't want to be, even though I went there when I wasn't feeling well. It was a place to go to feel better. Somehow now, doctor's offices weren't like that. They seemed more about hearing bad news or discussing uncomfortable procedures or debating treatment plans. As I looked at the toys, I wished to go back to that time.

"Susannah?" I heard from door number one.

"Yes," I said, startled, distracted by the toy that's in every medical waiting room, the one with the squiggly wires in different colors with the wood beads that kids supposedly move and watch slide down, even though I've never seen a kid actually play with this before.

"I'm Lucille, but you can call me Luci. I'll be with you in a second. Why don't you come on in and have a seat," she motioned to me. The waiting room filled with natural sunlight, and it was only then that I realized there were no windows where I was waiting, but her room had a wonderfully large, tinted window, a room bright enough that it didn't need a lamp.

I stood up, my knees shakier than I expected. My breath felt shallow and it stuck in my throat. I entered the room and scanned the seating options. There was the chair by the desk that was against the window, the desk signifying the boundary that meant this was Luci's chair. There was another chair next to the door I imagined was there for when extra seating was needed. Then there was the stereotypical couch, although it wasn't tufted leather but rather a pastel fabric that looked like it was from the 1980s. I sat on the end closest to the desk chair, setting my purse next to me and looking out the window, wishing I had gone for that walk on the Boulevard instead.

"Thank you for waiting. I was in a meeting and I just needed a moment before we got started," Luci explained as she closed the door.

"No problem." I replied.

She walked over to the desk chair and wrote a note on a pad. She set the pen down and then swiveled in my direction.

Silence.

I knew this meant it was time for me to talk, that I had to start. I explained everything, starting with my self-diagnosis of PTSD. Then I got into the details: my dad, who he was in the community, that day, the tree, *a thousand cardboard boxes*, the rocking, the surgery, the heart attack, his passing, my anger, the questions from people, storms, Florida, this October snowstorm, that tree, another *thousand cardboard boxes*, shaking. Most of the hour was used up explaining everything while Luci interjected "That's awful" and "How terrible" at each upsetting turn. I cried when I explained my dad died; it was something I hadn't verbalized in a while.

Not wanting this diagnosis, but wanting validation, I asked, "Am I right when I say I think I have PTSD?"

Luci nodded. "Yes, you have PTSD."

I knew it for years, but hearing it now made it feel real.

"I just want to get over this already. It's been fourteen years. I don't want the sound of trees ripping apart to bring back those memories. I'm lucky that I don't hear that every day, but I didn't even think I'd hear it again last month and that it would make me shake with anxiety and sadness. I don't want storms to make me nervous anymore. I don't want these things impacting my life. How do I make this stop? How do I get over this for good?"

Luci leaned in a little. "You don't."

I didn't expect to hear that. I thought I'd learn breathing techniques and whatever else that could break behavioral patterns. I was shocked, but instantly I felt lighter, as if the burden of fighting something was lifted. The fight to make it stop, to stop shaking, to stop crying, to stop bursts of anger, to make PTSD go away for good was ultimately not a battle worth fighting. What happened was part of the fabric of my being, a permanent wrinkle that no matter how hot the iron gets and how hard I pressed would always be there. It was that obvious: *Of course the sound of a tree ripping and falling is going to upset me . . . wouldn't it be odd if it didn't?*

"This doesn't mean it has to run your life," Luci reassured, "and let's talk more about that next time." The hour had already run over.

I made a follow-up appointment, but as I mulled this new idea that I would always have PTSD, I wasn't sure I even needed to talk to Luci again. *Stop fighting it. Move through it, and then let it go.* I left the session as my mind recalibrated. Her two words—*you don't*—echoed. I felt the change from those two words alone.

Feeling significantly stronger, I went to the follow-up anyway. This time, Mike came with me, sitting next to me on the couch with his arm resting on the back behind me. Luci thought it was important for him to understand my reactions and thoughts when the tree fell during the snowstorm, knowing that he would be the most likely person for me to turn to if a strong storm and *a thousand cardboard boxes* should happen again. I watched as Mike took it all in.

Luci caught on that I tend to be insightful. "What's helped you these past fourteen years?" she asked, knowing I had accomplished a lot during that time and not taken the path that started and continued with rocking. "Keep doing those things," she encouraged. We agreed that I was lucky that my biggest trigger has only happened a handful of times in my life, and the chances of it happening again were slim. My other trigger—thunderstorms—I needed to learn how to stop fighting my symptoms and instead move through them

I didn't make another follow-up appointment. Luci suggested calling her only if needed. After we left, Mike and I took a walk on the Boulevard.

CHAPTER 12

Wedding Crasher

SITTING CROSS-LEGGED ON THE FLOOR of my balcony facing the Gulf of Mexico, I breathed deeply . . . it was my wedding day. I woke up alone in my hotel room feeling calm but excited. This would be a big day, one of the most important ones of my life. I stretched forward, releasing tension in my lower back. I uncrossed my legs and moved my lower back upward, settling into downward dog. I've always loved this yoga pose. I love how it stretches every muscle fiber in my shoulders and elongates my back. I savored it for a few moments. I moved down into child's pose, then forward into cat pose and then slowly stood up.

Surya namaskar . . . Sun salutation. Inhale and sweep your arms outward and upward, stretching above your head. Exhale and bend forward deep into uttanasana. Inhale and arch your back upward. Exhale into plank pose. Inhale . . . chaturanga. Exhale . . . upward dog. Inhale . . . exhale . . . downward dog . . . stay in downward dog . . . my favorite pose. Inhale and look past your hands and step forward. Exhale . . . uttanasana. Inhale and come up, sweeping your arms overhead. Exhale . . . tadasana. I coached myself mentally through the regimen.

I repeated sun salutations two more times as the rain misted me through the screens. I could have done all the sun salutations I wanted, but they weren't going to change the weather. Tropical Storm Debbie decided to crash our wedding. She was packing lots of rain and high surf. For months, I had thought about our beach wedding. Uncle Bill was going to walk me down a trail through the dunes and sea grass onto the beach where a path of yellow, orange, and purple rose petals would lead the way to a bamboo canopy draped with white chiffon and tropical flowers. Mike would be under the bamboo canopy along with his best man, James, and my bridesmaids, Gayle and Julia. Our guests would be sitting in chairs facing the water, watching the ceremony while the sky lit up with color as the sun set, backlighting the pelicans as they dove for fish. The soft waves would play beautiful background music to our vows. Dolphins would swim by, giving us an unexpected delightful show. This is how I saw myself marrying Mike … on a perfect tropical summer evening.

For days, we knew Tropical Storm Debbie was coming. The chances for an amazing sunset slimmed as the forecast turned ugly. Thick clouds overcast, not a chance of color as the sun set, a sun we couldn't even tell where it was in the sky. I hoped for a clearing lasting just long enough for us to marry on the beach. I knew that might not happen.

I had several hours before we had to decide if we needed to change our plans. One thought repeated during my long yoga practice: *I'm marrying Mike.* I was happy for this day, but wishful. I knew my dad wouldn't walk me down the aisle, but as that moment approached I felt him missing more and more.

We specifically chose Captiva on the Florida coast for our wedding. Not only was it beautiful, it was also as convenient a destination wedding could be for most of our guests. When I was a senior in high school, my parents and I vacationed on neighboring Sanibel Island for a week. It was a wonderful trip for the three of us, our last hurrah together before I left the nest for college. Deciding to get married here made it feel like my dad was a part of it, knowing he had seen these Gulf views, swam in the warm water, and searched for beautiful shells on the beach.

I got dressed and headed to breakfast with Gayle. Then we went for a walk on the beach while Mike went fishing with Uncle Bill, his best man James, and a few other guests. It rained constantly, gradually becoming heavier and heavier. The waves in the normally calm Gulf crashed against the shore. We walked back to our rooms when we could no longer take getting wet. After I took a shower, I made my way to the spa. Gayle, Julia, and my future mother-in-law joined me in getting ready.

As the makeup artist was applying eye shadow, my wedding planner called. "We've been waiting all afternoon, hoping this rain would clear up, but the waves are so big that they're covering the entire beach. There's no way we can have the wedding on the beach," she reported.

The restaurant where our reception was to be held became our venue. Uncle Bill drove me and we waited in the car on the edge of the parking lot while the guests arrive. Months before, I asked him to walk me down the aisle. Uncle Bill and I are never at a loss of words for each other, but as we waited, I could feel what we were both thinking. As much as the rain had taken away the sunset, the rose petals on the sandy aisle, the dolphins, and all of the other elements I had envisioned for months leading up to the ceremony, while the rain poured heavily as we sat in the car waiting, those missing details didn't seem to matter.

"I think you should know that I really like Mike and you're marrying a really good guy," he said tiptoeing into tender territory.

"Thank you."

"And I know your dad would have really liked him too."

"I know." My dad would have loved Mike. They say girls marry their fathers, and Mike and my dad definitely had some similarities. They both enjoyed working in the yard. They both liked ice cream and indulging in certain foods. They both liked to laugh. They both carried themselves with integrity and wanted to help others all the time. Even the unique sound Mike made when he blew his nose was like my dad's. Later on, we discovered that the wedding ring Mike picked out was the exact same size and style as my dad's. They would have played golf, gone fishing, and enjoyed a beer afterward, possibly spending more time together on weekends than Mike and I would.

"I know this is not your ideal wedding," Uncle Bill pointed out, "but what matters most is you're marrying Mike."

"That's what's making this rain okay today," I replied.

Uncle Bill nodded.

Knock . . . knock. The photographer was at the car window. Uncle Bill rolled it down.

"It's time! We have a golf umbrella for you."

Uncle Bill took the umbrella, walked over to my door, and helped me out of the car.

"Well, this is it!" he said, excitedly.

This is it!

We made our way around puddles while the wedding photographer snapped away. This was the complete opposite of what I had imagined. The path that was supposed to be sand and sea grass was gravel and water. I couldn't help laughing.

I entered the restaurant and was greeted by the guitar player playing a tune I didn't recognize at all even though Mike and I had selected the play list. I turned towards the aisle, noticing it was really narrow. Rather than walking me by my side down the aisle with my arm in his, Uncle Bill followed me down the aisle holding my hand. To my left were everyone's faces, all standing and smiling, taking photos and dabbing tears. I felt it immediately . . . it didn't matter that this was not our amazing beach wedding, that the sand, the sunset, the pelicans, the waves, the rose petals, and the dolphins were missing. The best thing was something I neither planned for, nor expected: to be overpowered by the love that emanated from every single family member and friend.

It took only about ten steps for me to get to Mike. There was no room for Gayle and Julia to stand next to me, so they stood with James. Looking over to them, I could see into the kitchen where the staff was cooking up a storm of their own. I later learned that Gayle had discreetly turned to the chefs and asked them to be quiet. I brought my attention back to Mike and looked into his eyes. Instead of seeing the Gulf behind him, I noticed the restroom sign right above his head. I hid my laughter inside. The ceremony started. As I was listening to the wedding planner conduct our ceremony, Mike and I kept smiling at each other. Everyone remained standing throughout the ceremony, as if everyone wanted to be a part of our wedding party.

"Have patience with each other, for storms will come, and they will go quickly . . . "

The room erupted with laughter.

We said our vows and were pronounced husband and wife.

We took pictures on the beach in the pouring rain. James covered us with an umbrella and jumped in and out of shots covering and uncovering us to keep us as dry as possible while he got drenched. He carried my shoes and cleaned them off when we got back to the restaurant, earning him the title of the *best* best man ever. He treated us to a fabulous speech, which was followed by more amazing words from Gayle and Uncle Bill. Mike enjoyed the New York strip steak while I had the yummiest mahi mahi. The best key lime pie in the entire world served as our wedding cake. We laughed a lot, ate a lot, drank a lot, and kissed a lot as our guests kept pinging their wine glasses. Tropical Storm Debbie did her thing outside. For having crashed our wedding, she gave us one awesome gift: an amazing lightning show over the Gulf—the first time I had enjoyed lightning in a very long time.

CHAPTER 13

Superstorm Sandy

IT WAS SUPPOSED TO BE ONLY a hurricane, as if a hurricane can be *only* something. For several days, meteorologists predicted the unprecedented. The storm of the century, one of a scale we had never seen before and may never see again. Their coverage wasn't dramatic. It was urgent. Direct. The meteorologists actually look scared. They weren't crying wolf this time, as much as we could hope that Mother Nature would outsmart the experts and prove them wrong again. They were right this time.

Three days before the storm, on Facebook I happened upon a link to an article that described why Hurricane Sandy, as it was named before it got its title upgrade, would be worse than Hurricane Irene. It compared the two storms, concluding that this storm was much larger in size, slower in speed, and hitting New Jersey during a full moon over several high tides. Storm surges and strength were explained in detail, reinforcing what the meteorologists were saying: It was not worth taking this lightly. It hit me that this could be the strongest storm I'd ever been through.

I emailed the article to Mike, who immediately understood my concern. We had several days to prepare to minimize the potential for damage to our house and ourselves. Mike focused on securing the house, while I rescheduled patients and made sure I had the contact information for everyone that was scheduled for the next two weeks. On my way home, I went to the store to stock up on water and food. To my surprise, the shelves were packed with supplies. I expected them to be empty or at least thin. I wondered if people were unaware, in disbelief, in denial, or still tired from the effects from Hurricane Irene and the October snowstorm, both only a year before.

I loaded my cart with enough water to sustain me, Mike, and the cats for four days. I would have purchased more, but the cart so heavy with twelve gallons of water that I had to lean into it just to get it down the aisle. I filled the rest of the cart with boxes of crackers, granola bars, raisins, and nuts. The haul was heavy enough that my car sank after I loaded it up.

By the time I came home, Mike had already completed a bunch of things that were on his list. His biggest and most important task was stockpiling gas for the generator, a device we purchased soon after the October snowstorm. Mike tested it several times to make sure it worked. He also had a chain and lock ready, since rumor had it that generators were stolen right from people's property out of desperation after the October snowstorm. In addition to stockpiling gas, Mike ordered a siphon so that we could pull gas from our cars. With each gallon of gas that Mike saved, he calculated how many hours without power it would last us. The generator supplied an hour of power for every half gallon, so fourteen gallons of gas stored in cans would give us twenty-eight hours of energy. If we ran the generator for a few hours each morning and evening, we were good for about seven days before we would need to siphon gas from our cars.

Every day before the storm, Mike asked me how I was feeling about it. The obvious answer was "Not great," but surprisingly, I wasn't anxious. I stayed in the moment, which was much better than imagining what might come. I vacuumed the house, folded laundry, read a book, scrolled through Facebook, and kept the days leading up to the storm as normal as possible. Distractions from what was coming, and reminders from therapy to myself—*you don't*. I told myself that whatever happened I would not fight it.

We were prepared for the storm two days before it was supposed to start. We checked in with friends and family to see how they were doing. We were most concerned for Uncle Bill and Susan. Their primary residence was on the Upper West Side in Manhattan, but their second home, that wonderful house on the Sound in Connecticut where I had collected so much sea glass, was just feet away from the water, making it extremely vulnerable. They'd been through storms and nor'easters before, sometimes experiencing minor damage, but this superstorm had the potential to wash away their three-story house. Mike asked if they needed an extra hand moving things out of their house to store in a safer location. They were thankful for the offer, but felt prepared enough. There was only so much they could do.

I knew an acupuncture relief clinic was going to be needed after the storm. I emailed Toni and asked her if she would be interested in doing a clinic with me. She had been thinking the same thing and had the acupuncture supply kit from Hurricane Irene ready. I emailed Acupuncturists Without Borders to let them know that Toni and I were prepared.

The day before the storm Mike double checked everything on the list and made sure our gas tanks were full. We enjoyed an afternoon dinner so we could go to bed early, figuring the next day was going to be long and stressful. Just as we finished eating, an idea came to mind. If we lost power, there was not much for me to do to occupy myself. I knew that once the storm came, I wouldn't want to think about what was happening outside. I would need a distraction while the wind whipped and the trees swayed, something that would require a lot of time and perhaps be a project that I could not finish in one day. Counted cross stitching, a rather old-fashioned handicraft, came to mind. This involves creating an image on fabric using different colors of floss. The image is mapped out on a diagram complete with boxes filled with shapes that coordinate with the color floss that should be used. It was a craft I had done as a teenager and enjoyed a lot. When you start stitching the floss, it's important to keep checking the diagram and counting the number of boxes to determine the number of stitches that need to be done; otherwise a mistake could mess up the entire pattern. It requires a lot of focus to move between the diagram and the project itself, but it's very satisfying once the white material starts to produce a beautiful image. A perfect storm distraction.

It was getting dark and Mike was putting the dinner dishes in the dishwasher. "I need to get a craft project for tomorrow."

Mike looked at me with surprise, knowing that the first bands of the storm were a few hours away, but I knew he understood what I meant.

"Okay, let's go," he said.

I hadn't bought a counted cross stitch pattern in years, but I remembered that Michaels carried them. We went to the nearest store and went right to the needlework section, or what I thought was the needlework section. I searched the aisle, but could not find any kits. After walking up and down every aisle, scanning every shelf, I still didn't see any kits. I asked someone who worked in the store where I could find the counted cross stitch kits and she pointed to where they should be, but there were none left. Either everyone had the same idea as me and all the kits had been sold or this type of craft was so outdated that Michaels didn't even care if it was well stocked. Seeing that they did not have a lot of shelf space for the counted cross stitch kits made me think the latter might be true, which made me concerned that I may not get a kit at all even if we tried going to a different Michaels.

"Let's try Joann Fabric," I told Mike as we left the parking lot, happy that I remembered this other craft store I hadn't been to in over two decades. It was getting late and I hoped the store wasn't closed for the day . . . or for good. I wished I thought of this sooner and gotten a kit without having to run around now. My last hope was Joann Fabrics, and luckily, we got there an hour before closing and they had kits . . . only they were kits with really cutesy, countrified, outdated patterns . . . not exactly my style. I flipped through the different options, all the while kicking myself that I didn't think to order one online so I could choose a pattern that was really cool and modern, if counted cross stitch could *ever* be modern. Most of the kits didn't appeal to me except for one animal alphabet kit that was clearly intended for a nursery.

"This will do," I said as I grabbed it and went to the counter.

Tilting his head as if unsure, "Well, it seems like it's designed for a baby," Mike noted.

"Well, one day we'll have a baby and it can go in the baby's room."

Mike knew it wasn't the time to have the kids talk. I purchased the kit and we headed back to the car.

"Anything else before we head home?" Mike double checked.

"No, let's just go home."

It was dark out, the first gusts of wind and rain started. We went to bed right after getting home. Wide awake, both of us. Minds racing, wondering what tomorrow would be like, picturing something we'd never experienced. Trees blowing with the wind, rain crashing against the roof . . . *How far could it go? How strong would it be? What would happen?* We tossed and turned all night. Having seen on the news so many pictures from around the world of areas destroyed by what we knew to be the worst storms at the time, it was hard not to imagine this storm adding to those images. I closed my eyes and thought about . . . what else . . . the beach. *Warm sand. Seagulls. Ocean spray. Blue skies.* I finally fell asleep.

We woke up to gray skies, rain, and a little wind. Assuming we'd lose power later that day, we showered and ate breakfast. The TV remained on, reporters stationed at various locations across the Tri-State Area. Through rain and wind, they repeated the same phrases over and over—*storm surges, widespread flooding, wind damage, power outages*—until 7:00 am when *The Today Show* started, opening with a live shot of Uncle Bill and Susan's Connecticut house.

"Mike! Look! That's the Connecticut house!"

The shot cut away before Mike could look, but then seconds later it reappeared.

"Look! Look! There it is!"

"Oh wow, yeah!" Mike exclaimed. "That's the Connecticut house!"

"I have to call Uncle Bill and Susan."

I got Susan on the phone. I could hear her telling Uncle Bill to switch the channel. It looked like a reporter was on the sandbar covering the conditions with a second camera showing a live shot of the house. Boards covered the windows, protecting this wonderful house as best as possible. It looked scared. As much as Uncle Bill and Susan had prepared, I can't imagine they were ready to see footage of their house on TV. There is a balance between wanting to know and being better off not knowing. It gave me a whole new perspective for anyone who has ever lost a home or experienced a traumatic event that was caught on camera, something seemingly so common in this day and age, an element I'm glad didn't come with *a thousand cardboard boxes.*

After talking with Uncle Bill and Susan, I began my counted cross stitch, my plan for a continuous distraction. The pattern consisted of the alphabet with an animal next to its respective starting letter. It was broken down into boxes for each letter and animal, which was perfect, because I could focus on one box at a time and feel accomplished as I completed boxes. As a distraction, it worked. Every once in a while, the wind picked up, growing to a roar, but I only noticed it by the time it ceased. I was busy counting stitches, thinking, *Three up, four over, and then stitch five squares,* as the wind gusted, drawing my attention outside to what was happening, only to see that the gust died down. I'd turn my attention back to my craft, thinking, *Okay, so that was four up and three over or the other way around . . .* as I glanced back at the diagram.

The bands brought moments of deceptive stillness, the rain only a drizzle, the wind barely a breeze. At these times, I looked out the window up at the sky. Turbulent clouds. These were times where I stepped away from my counted cross stitching to give my eyes a rest while watching the clouds dance. Mike remained vigilant while we still had power, watching the radar on TV. When the radar showed a strong band moving closer, I returned to my stitching to wait it out. Other distractions evolved throughout the day: playing cards, reading articles online, playing with the cats, long conversations. Mike periodically interjected into my solo activities to ask me how I was doing. For all of the hype, my body felt relaxed like any other day. Amazingly calm. I stayed in that zone.

From our hill, we saw flashes from transformers exploding atop telephone poles. We knew it would be our turn soon for the lights to go out. A few flashes later, and we were next. No silence like the October snowstorm. Instead we heard the whistling of the wind, the creaks of swaying trees. By candlelight, I continued with my counted cross stitching, struggling to see the pattern. Mike finally stood up, opened the basement door, and closed it behind him. I heard his footsteps go down the wooden staircase followed by a squeak from the garage door. Looking out the window, I watched him start the generator. Life returned to the house, the silence broken by beeps and hums of appliances and everything else that keeps a house alive. With the generator going, we could use the refrigerator, shower, toilet, and a few outlets, and turn on some lights. A cozy feeling returned. Electricity felt like a luxury.

Nearly pitch black outside, and without the TV reports, the strength of the storm could only be measured in sound, which grew louder. My eyes and brain were tired from stitching and looking at the pattern. Mike was out of things to do. Simultaneously, we looked at each other, sensing immediately that neither of us wanted to go to bed but we also didn't want to listen to the storm all night.

"Why don't I shut off the generator and we go up-stairs and watch a movie on my laptop in bed," Mike suggested. "It's fully charged."

"That sounds perfect," I replied, relieved by his idea. We hadn't planned on watching a movie during the storm, but Mike had movies already downloaded and ready to watch on his computer. Mike shut off the generator and secured it inside the garage while I got ready for bed. The wind continued to strengthen, sounding louder upstairs. We brushed our teeth quicker than usual. As I took the throw pillows off the bed and Mike set up his laptop, I thought of the cats.

"I think the cats should sleep with us tonight," I suggested, knowing how good they were during the October snowstorm. However, this was a different cat scenario. Penny had crossed over the "rainbow bridge" ten months before. Since then, we'd adopted Lucky, a rambunctious though absolutely lovable kitten. Gizmo and Lucky acted like brothers, snuggling nearly every day, and working as a team. They knew how to get in trouble together. We tried allowing Gizmo and Lucky to sleep with us a few times before, but it had never worked out. One would crawl under the covers, getting in the way. While that one was under the covers, the other one would be constantly walking all over the bed and us and pouncing on him. Then Gizmo usually would decide he wanted to climb onto the dresser in Mike's closet and knock things over. Then one of them would start meowing. Then they both would want to walk all over us. Then one would put his wet nose in our ears. We wished they'd settle down and sweetly snuggle with us, but it never worked out that way.

Mike looked at me and considered my thought.

"I would feel more comfortable knowing they're with us in case something happens and we need to get out quickly," I explained.

Without hesitation, he walked around the bed and opened the door. "Come in boys! You're in luck! You guys get to sleep with us tonight!" Gizmo and Lucky bounded in, landing at the foot of the bed curled together, as if that was their plan all along.

We got in bed, careful not to kick the cats. Mike scrolled through his downloads. He had dozens of movies ready to watch, but many of these movies were rather deep and dark. Great movies, such as *The Hurt Locker* and *The Boy in the Striped Pajamas*, but not the kinds of movies that mask chaos outside. There were a bunch of action type movies, but I wanted something without violence, feeling the storm was violent enough. He had many animated films but they weren't very long, and we figured the longer the movie the longer our attention turned away from what was happening outside. The only option was *The Notebook*, which we had seen before together.

"Let's watch *The Notebook*," I said.

"But we've watched that already."

"So, let's watch it again. It's just over two hours long. It'll keep us occupied while the storm is really bad."

It was getting very bad. The wind roared louder. After a particularly strong gust, I glanced over at Mike and I could tell from the look in his eye that he was nervous too. We knew the worst was coming. What we didn't anticipate was the worst happening overnight, in the dark. The gusts grew stronger, the rain harder. Scarier and scarier, with no idea how long it would last.

The movie was a great escape. A love story was unfolding before us, the opposite of what was happening outside. Gizmo and Lucky slept on the bed, uninterested in the movie, happy to be near us. It was as if they knew it was scary outside, yet they somehow managed to fall asleep, barely lifting their heads with each wind gust. All of us curled together, helping each other stay calm while Sandy's worst rain bands slammed outside. The wind ripped across the roof like a freight train. Mike and I exchanged worried looks, wondering what it would take for our trees to uproot, what it would take for my car to flip over, what it would take for our house to blow apart . . . but each time the wind stopped and the house still stood. Back to watching the movie, this pattern repeating itself: wind, fear, calm, *We're still here.* The cats joined the rhythm. Then just when we thought we heard the strongest gust ever, a stronger one followed. Sometimes, it felt like it penetrated through the house, trying to swirl its energy into everything and everyone. My mind focused on the movie, suppressing its desire to race and flash.

Midnight. The movie was over. We were exhausted, but Sandy wasn't ready for bed. If anything, she was ready to rave. The wind was stronger than the one that created *a thousand cardboard boxes*. I wanted to sleep, to prevent my mind from going back to the porch, the tree, my mom's car, and the emergency lights. A new pattern emerged of drifting off to sleep, being startled by a strong gust, thinking of the porch, and taking deep breaths while Mike held me, then both of us drifting again. More repetitions: strong gust, *the car*, deep breaths, sleep . . . strong gust, *the ambulance*, deep breaths, sleep. But I didn't fight the pattern. Normal. I bet I wasn't the only one in the Tri-State Area quietly shaking in bed.

GIZMO AND LUCKY BEHAVED all night. No sun, but clouds brightened, waking us up. It was still stormy outside, but clearly the worst was over. I looked around the bedroom. It all looked the same. Mike got up and looked out the window. Aside from leaves and sticks throughout the yard, it was also the same. Every tree stood tall.

We went downstairs. The dining room, living room, kitchen . . . all the same. Mike looked out the French door. "Oh shit!"

"What's the matter?"

"Look! A roof shingle!"

We had a green roof, the only one on our street, and there lying neatly on the ground was one green roof shingle. Mike unlocked the French door and we stepped outside.

"Maybe that's the only one," I hoped.

"No look, there's more," Mike said, pointing to more shingles a few yards away. Surveying our side yard, he found more.

"Let's walk up the hill," I suggested. "We'll get a better view of the roof."

We walked up and glanced back at the roof, but nothing seemed out of place.

"Let's keep walking up," I said. "We'll get a better view up higher."

Up higher with a better view, still no large sections missing, no obvious damage.

"Maybe they're from the front of the house?" Mike wondered, since we only had a view of the back. Then, he noticed. "Oh, I see where they came off. They're from the ridge vent."

Mike was right. All along the peak of the roof half of the shingles were missing.

"I hope we didn't get water in the attic," Mike said, running inside to check.

I stayed in the yard, slowly searching for roof shingles, remembering that it's technically not over, yet I'm standing outside. Intact. I picked up the green shingles, stacking them next to the house.

"Good, there's no water damage in the attic."

"Do you think we're going to need a new roof?"

"Eventually yes, but if we didn't get water damage from this storm, then we should be good for a while."

Intact. Exactly how I felt.

CHAPTER 14

The Shore

BEYOND A HURRICANE . . . A SUPERSTORM.

Compared to so many, we were living in luxury, thankful for every bit of it. We were without power for four days. We ran the generator in the morning while we got ready for work and then ran it at night for a few hours. It made all the difference, so much better than having nothing at all. We didn't have TV and we learned very little from reading Facebook and news websites from our cell phones.

I called Uncle Bill. He and Susan were completely fine in Manhattan. They never lost power on the Upper West Side, the day before only seemed like a bad rain storm. He knew nothing about what happened in Connecticut. Susan's brother lived in the same town high up on a hill and could not get close enough to check on the house due to road closures and flooding. They were hoping for the best, but expecting the worst, with not a single thing they could do about it at this point. Like us, they were thankful they had a home and would be more so if it was unscathed.

Mike and I ventured out to check on my office. No power, but no damage. Most of downtown Boonton looked messy, but fine. Tons of trees were down in the surrounding communities. Hardly anyone had power. But the damage was recoverable.

The next day, I went to work at Morristown Memorial Hospital, a position I had taken in addition to my private practice, the goal of gaining experience in a hospital setting. It was outpatient work and I knew my patient schedule would be extremely light. Knowing that the hospital had power, I decided to go to work early with my computer to use the Wi-Fi signal to get online and communicate with my private practice patients.

It was early, about 6:30 am, quiet except for a few nurses and hospital employees sitting in the waiting area, all looking at the TV, something I'd never seen them do collectively before. It didn't occur to me that

I would be able to watch the news at the hospital. What I saw on the screen was mind blowing.

A reporter in a helicopter revealed Mantoloking, New Jersey, a very nice beach community on the barrier islands, now only identifiable by the words below the image. Many times, I drove along Route 35 North after spending the day at Island Beach State Park just south of Seaside Park, a scenic way of avoiding the Garden State Parkway traffic for a few miles. It's lined with beautiful homes right on the beach, many of them located in Mantoloking, dream properties that I always wondered if I'd ever be so lucky to own. Those luxury homes were now sand and debris with pockets of small fires from compromised gas lines. It was a disaster.

A nurse walked in and sat down. "Oh my god," she said.

"It's bad, isn't it," said another nurse.

"That's in Mantoloking?"

"It looks like it."

"My house is in Mantoloking."

I could immediately feel her energy upon her discovery. Knowing how hard the staff works at this hospital, I imagined she spent the night here tending to patients with no idea what was happening at home until now. This was her first look.

"It's a beachfront house. What are all of those fires?"

"Apparently the gas lines caught fire and it's just moving down the gas line."

"Oh my god! Oh my god! I can't believe this. My home is there!"

It was hard not to feel it sink in for her. If her home wasn't completely gone already, it was now in danger of burning down. She collapsed in her seat, her eyes glued to the TV, her hand over her mouth. Trauma was hitting her.

I texted Toni to check in on her, relaying what I was watching on the news. She was fine, but had no power. We were in agreement: If we were going to set up acupuncture clinics with Acupuncturists Without Borders, we needed to be down the shore.

WE GOT POWER BACK hours before *Hurricane Sandy: Coming Together*, the telethon organized by

NBC. We were lucky considering millions were still in the dark. Mike and I really wanted to watch it.

Christina Aguilera beautifully opened the show, followed by Matt Lauer talking about the storm and making a point that tugged at me: "One of the great ironies of this benefit concert is that the people we're trying to help can't watch it."

Sting sang one of my favorite songs, "Message in a Bottle."

The obvious messages put in a bottle: clothing, food, blankets. What about emotional support? Stress relief? All I could think about was anxiety, flashbacks and whether anyone was crying, shaking, or rocking back and forth. I imagined *SOS* meant more than just clothing, food, and blankets.

MARIA HAD STAYED in her house in Lavallette. She'd lived there for the last several decades, a small Cape Cod-style home just a few houses away from the beach. She had thought she had seen every storm, every hurricane, every tropical storm, and every nor'easter, which is why she stayed. The worst that had ever happened was minor flooding. A retired senior citizen, roughly seventy years of age, who loved the shore and her neighbors, she lived alone and on a fixed income, living her dream, near the beach. She had no idea that Sandy would destroy her dream life.

As the water rose in her house, she made her way upward to the second floor, bringing with her a few supplies to last her until she was rescued. When it became apparent to her that help wouldn't come until the next day, and with the waters continuing to rise, she climbed into her attic. She spent the evening there during the height of the storm while the first and second floors of her home swirled with ocean water, the wind and rain pounding against her roof.

The next morning, the Army came in and rescued her from her house. They drove her and a few others to another truck that took them to a shelter. Maria was now homeless. She had lost everything. She told me and Toni her story as she received acupuncture at our Acupuncturists Without Borders relief clinic in Brick. Normally, during our clinics we suggest that everyone rests quietly to help maintain a healing atmosphere, but today everyone needed to share their stories. By far, Maria's was the worst.

All day, Toni and I fought back tears. It was our first day in Brick at the Police Athletic League (PAL) building doing our clinic. We had a large team of AWB volunteers securing locations for clinics, spreading the word and providing acupuncture. Some of our volunteers, including Toni, were displaced or had damage to second homes. Toni's family home, which had been handed down from generation to generation in Seaside Park, now sat slightly damaged among a neighborhood of destruction. Some volunteers were living in shelters. Some had a significant number of their patients affected by the storm, which threatened their practices. Regardless, everyone was eager to help, willing to put their needs aside and create something positive out of a bad situation. Two weeks after the storm, we had our first clinic up and running in Point Pleasant at St. Mary's by-the-Sea Episcopal Church. Toni and I knew that the shore needed multiple clinic locations given the widespread damage. Our second clinic came a week later in Brick.

We worked alongside Operation Brick Food Relief (OBFR), a grassroots relief effort started by a handful of people who wanted to make a difference. In a very short time, this small group had recruited hundreds of volunteers, secured use of the kitchen at the local PAL, and had received who knows how many tons of donated food. OBFR served hundreds of hot meals to people at the Brick PAL and delivered thousands of meals to anyone in the Brick area that needed them. They did this every day.

The scene at OBFR was a controlled busy. Hundreds of people volunteered, working together like a well-oiled machine, as if they had been doing this for years. Long buffet lines, lots of tables filled with people getting a hot meal, music pumping to keep the energy up. Everyone working hard, giving their time, many of the leaders spending extremely long hours at the PAL making sure as many people as possible were helped. The best example of the human spirit I've ever witnessed.

The OBFR organizers were excited to see us. They walled off an area for us to set up our clinic, large enough for us to treat ten people at a time. As we set up our supplies, people's curiosity peaked.

"What are you offering?"

"Free acupuncture for help with stress relief."

That answer usually brought two general types of responses: "Oh! That's so wonderful! Can I have a treatment?" or "Acupuncture? Does it really help?"

Maria was in the second, more skeptical category, but with dark circles under her exhausted, watery eyes and her posture hunched as if she had the weight of the world on her shoulders it was clear she needed some type of stress relief. She didn't smile at all, looking like she had been constantly crying for days. We managed to convince her to try it.

The acupuncture treatment protocol that we use in AWB clinics is very simple, but can have a very profound effect. It is a five-needle treatment done entirely on the ear. An entire system of treating the body using ear acupuncture maps out acupuncture points like an upside down human fetus—the head mostly represented in the ear lobe with the rest of the body curling upwards. Using ear acupuncture allows people to receive a very comprehensive treatment without needing to get undressed or lie down on a treatment table. That way, several people can be treated quickly, safely, and efficiently while seated in chairs in a group setting.

All of the points used in this protocol for stress relief are powerful, but the first point can sometimes have the biggest effect. For Maria, that was the case. She immediately felt a sensation in her body when it was inserted. Often times, it's a warming sensation that gradually builds and helps relax the body. At first, this sensation made her nervous, so we proceeded slowing, moving to the next point only when she was comfortable. Color returned to her face and her eyes brightened. She still felt nervous, but she was actually looking better. She rested quietly for a few minutes, until she felt the need to start talking. Then she asked the others getting treatment how the storm was for them. Some had also stayed home, also been rescued by the Army. Like Maria, one sought shelter in an attic. All were without homes and living in different shelters. All had rough stories, but Maria's sounded the scariest.

I couldn't imagine being in an attic with the ocean crashing against the house and the winds blowing as fast as they were. Maria said she prayed the entire time, the only thing she could do.

Forty minutes of resting and Maria was ready for us to take the needles out. Her face was much pinker, the circles under her eyes nearly gone, the sadness greatly erased from her face.

"How do you feel?" I asked.

"You were right. I do feel a lot better. When are you coming back?"

We gave Maria our clinic schedule for Point Pleasant and Brick. At that point, we offered free acupuncture six days per week between these two clinics. We were gaining popularity among people who received treatments, helping people who were stressed out about their homes, their jobs, their entire lives. So many felt significantly better after treatment. Many wanted to know when they could come back for another one. We were just beginning to make a major impact on people when unfortunately, like many relief efforts, things changed quickly.

I arrived at St. Mary's in Point Pleasant and was told that all area churches were consolidating their efforts in order to better serve people. Any resources that people needed were now at St. Paul's United Methodist Church in Bay Head. We contacted that church and set a date to start treating there, which unfortunately wasn't as immediate as we had hoped.

About a week after that, Toni and I drove together to Brick for our Saturday clinic. We walked in and discovered that hardly anyone was there, the buffet line was very short, and very little food was available. For whatever reason, the PAL was kicking out OBFR. It caused a local outrage, making headlines, but the PAL didn't budge, forcing OBFR to scramble for another location. That was our busiest clinic and now it was in jeopardy. We decided to focus on developing the Bay Head clinic and I drove down for the first clinic to lead the volunteers.

Chi Nguyen wanted to volunteer as soon as she heard about the AWB clinics. Her acupuncture clinic was in a beautiful location in Bay Head overlooking the water. She had prepared for the storm by removing some items from her clinic, but had no idea then that ten feet of water would come inside and destroy everything. She lost her entire office. Not only that; nearly all of the business owners she knew in the area, people she had spent years building relationships with, also lost everything. Additionally, a large portion of her patient population was greatly affected by the storm. Of all of the AWB volunteers we had in New Jersey, Chi was the only one whose clinic was destroyed.

I could not imagine losing my clinic. My acupuncture practice was like a baby to me. I conceived it, planned it, opened it, financed it, and grew it. It had taken many hours of blood, sweat, and tears to get it where it was. It supported my life and my future. Chi had been in practice for over a decade in her office, probably putting in the same kind of energy I put into my practice. It must have been paradise treating people while having a view of the bay, a dream practice setting. For Chi, that was all gone. I felt terrible for her.

I knew Chi really wanted to volunteer with the clinics, but I was a little hesitant. I wasn't sure where she was with her own trauma from the storm. I could not imagine pulling myself together to volunteer while knowing my practice was in such limbo. That is where Chi and I were different. Upon meeting her I could see she was still smiling despite everything that had happened. She had a bright light behind her eyes, demonstrating genuine happiness to be at this clinic. She yearned to help others, not wanting the storm to take that away from her too. Sandy had taken away her clinic, but she refused to let it take away her passion. She knew that by helping others and doing what she loved to do, something that she was unsure how she would do in the future, she would ultimately help herself.

Chi was a great volunteer and one of the most compassionate people I have ever met. She talked to so many about acupuncture and how it can help, drawing people in to give acupuncture a try. Some knew her already, such as the fellow business owners in her community, who were in the same boat as her and starting over from scratch. Some were her patients, facing similar struggles. I could see that with every connection she made she felt happier. Helping these people made her happy and made something positive come out of a terrible storm.

A FEW WEEKS LATER, Maria came to the Bay Head clinic. She had been a regular at the Brick clinic, but because of OBFR's turmoil with the Brick PAL, which caused confusion for many who had received treatments at our Brick clinic, I hadn't seen her in weeks. I was so happy to see Maria, happy that she had found us and wanted more treatments. She sat down on the church pew. Before we got started, I sat down in front of her and turned to face her. "How are you doing, Maria?" I asked, checking in.

More tears welled in her eyes than I'd ever seen before. For a few moments she couldn't speak.

"Oh, Maria," I said as I put a hand on her shoulder.

"It's just been so tough," she explained. "I've been moving from shelter to shelter this whole time and where I'm supposed to go to get food keeps changing."

"You haven't been able to stay in one place?" I asked.

"No. I was in Toms River for a while. Then Monmouth. Then Freehold. I'm supposed to go somewhere else soon, but I don't know where yet."

I could tell she was fighting her feelings, not wanting to break down. I could only guess that either she was tired of crying all the time or nervous that once she started she wouldn't be able to stop.

"What kind of aid are you getting?" I asked.

"I haven't gotten much except for a place to sleep and meals sometimes."

"What do you mean *sometimes?*"

"Sometimes I don't get meals."

"You mean you go without eating?"

"Yes."

"How often does that happen?"

"Well, I'm eating every day, but sometimes I only get one meal."

I could not believe what I was hearing. It was now two months after Superstorm Sandy and she was really struggling.

"So, you haven't gotten any FEMA aid or any donation money or insurance money?"

"Nothing yet. FEMA is hard to deal with. Some of the documents they want got washed away in the storm. Insurance hasn't come through yet and it sounds like I won't get much if it does because they're saying the storm was an "act of God." I haven't received any donation money, just some clothes and food."

My heart sank. Here Maria was, in her seventies, alone, having spent the worst of the storm in her attic, and now she was caught up in red tape. I wondered where the millions of dollars that people donated had gone. Where was her support system? Her SOS hadn't been answered, nor did it seem like it would be.

"I'm just so afraid that I'll never be able to return to my house. I just want to go home, but there's no home to go to, and I don't know if there will ever be a home to go to." She couldn't keep the tears back anymore, letting them fall gently.

I didn't know what to say, so I said what came to me, trying not to let myself get caught up in her tears so that I wouldn't cry with her, at least not outwardly.

"Maria, I wish I could give you a home, and I wish it could be built where your old home was, and I wish you didn't have to worry about meals or money. I wish I could do all of these things for you, but I can't. But what I can do is help you feel a little better."

I wished for all of these things for the tens of thousands of people in the same position as her. Between her retirement savings, social security checks, and whatever money would eventually trickle in from insurance or FEMA, I feared Maria and many others might spend the rest of their lives struggling just for basic necessities, struggles that were on top of whatever traumatic stress so many were visibly carrying that it was impossible to ignore. It was a reality devastating to imagine and Maria had to live it.

She nodded and I proceeded with her acupuncture treatment. Each time she received acupuncture, she could only tolerate a few needles at a time. For this treatment, she was able to handle the entire protocol. Like previous times, the color returned to her face and her demeanor calmed. She rested with the needles for close to thirty minutes. During her rest, she asked me if I knew of where she could get free meals close to Freehold. I did some research on my phone and was able to find three options for her, which I wrote down and gave to her along with my card.

"If you need anything at all, Maria, I want you to call me. My number is right on this card. Anything at all, please don't hesitate to call me. I will do my best to help you."

She thanked me as she got up. That was the last time I spoke with Maria.

Whenever I think about Superstorm Sandy and the work I did with Acupuncturists Without Borders, I think about Maria. I wonder if she's found a new home or was somehow able to rebuild. I wonder if a

year after the storm she was still displaced, still looking for food, still fighting FEMA and her insurance
company. More than anything, I wonder if she's had
moments of joy. Has she been able to smile? Has she
been able to find new friends? Has she been able to
recover from the traumatic effects from the storm,
even just a little bit?

Ultimately, Superstorm Sandy was a gift for me in
that I discovered what works for me in coping with
my PTSD, a lesson I don't ever want to repeat, but
know that I can if I have to. The lesson that I didn't
expect to take from the storm is that as a society we
need to do more for people suffering through traumatic events. Operation Brick Food Relief was a
grassroots effort that helped a tremendous number
of people in need, people who were still living in their
homes with missing walls and roofs without power or
heat because they refused to leave, instead putting all
of their energy into repairing storm damage. These
people told the OBFR volunteers how valuable those
meals were in helping them feel better, not just from
nutrition, but also in lifting their spirits up, feeling
touched by their generosity, a major step in helping
people recover from emotional trauma. Many of

these people looked forward to seeing OBFR volunteers deliver meals. It was an incredibly positive moment during their darkest days, a moment to connect with compassionate strangers and feel gratitude for a hot meal. The OBFR volunteers were driven not only to feed people; they also knew their efforts were helping people begin to get their lives back together, physically and emotionally.

Acupuncturists Without Borders started out as a grassroots effort and our New Jersey team and several other teams throughout the Tri-State Area were able to help people begin to recover from their emotional trauma. These efforts started from nothing, driven by people with a passion to help others as directly as possible, resulting in a huge difference for more people than most ever thought possible. As a society, we need to create and support more of these kinds of efforts following a disaster. They are what help give people the momentum to get back on their feet, to start smiling again, to start living again, reminding us of the amazing kindness, generosity, and strength of the human spirit. FEMA and other larger, more established organizations often times need to do their due diligence to make sure their funds are not abused, which often leads to the creation of red tape, making coping with trauma that much harder. In the interim, it's the grassroots efforts that can make the biggest impact to start.

UNCLE BILL AND SUSAN had to wade through nearly waist-deep water to get to their house in Connecticut. Thankfully, it was still standing. Unfortunately, they sustained some damage: a one-inch gap had developed between the siding and the foundation, which allowed water to seep into their first floor. They also lost their entire yard. Compared to others in their neighborhood, including a house that floated into the bay and moved in and out with the tides, they were extremely lucky, very relieved, and tremendously thankful. Still, they were very upset for their neighbors, many of whom had extensive damage. One day while cleaning up, a smile was put back on their faces when a small group of kids approached Uncle Bill in his driveway and offered him a home-made chocolate chip cookie.

CHAPTER 15

Peace

SAND DOLLARS DOTTED OUR PATH as we walked along the water's edge. For whatever reason, nature chose Manresa State Beach on Monterey Bay in California to litter its shoreline with these amazing treasures from the ocean. Gayle had brought us here specifically to find them. I'd never found one in nature before, but we picked up dozens that day. Their dried skeletons, their beauty left behind. We left the ones with the purple fuzz alone—their coating indicated life remained—but the others we sought.

"Aunt Soozie! Look!" exclaimed my five-year-old niece, Rowan, as she handed me a sand dollar for safekeeping.

"Wow! So big! Did you find it?" I asked her. She nodded, shining a big grin.

She ran off toward my mom and grabbed her hand. My mom, bundled up in her hoodie, safe from the cool bay breezes, moved her gaze away from the horizon toward Rowan and smiled. She looks just like her ... and just like me. The first time I saw Rowan, she was five-weeks old and nursing her mother. Seeing only the back of her head, I saw myself. Still now, her back was just like mine. She had the same carefree innocence I had at her age. Gayle walked along the water as she searched for more sand dollars. Amy, her partner, balanced the rest of Rowan's findings in her hands. Mike engrossed himself in photographing the surf, the cliffs, the found treasures, and all of us.

I breathed ... and felt it. My inner life force vibrated stronger than ever within my surroundings every time I visited Capitola, the best corner in the entire state of California. Colorful. Sweet. Chill. Flowers constantly bloomed at every turn. Eucalyptus trees radiated their wonderful scent, which simultaneously invigorated and cleared my head. Kelp beds floated on the water. Sea otters popped up among the sea weed, the females held their pups on their bellies.

Sea lions swam among the surfers as they waited to catch a wave. Hundreds of pelicans dove for fish as they came upon a school. Dolphins leaped up and mirrored the joy everyone felt on the beach. Seeing the people who packed Capitola Beach, their towels and beach chairs speckling the sand with color, the more vibrancy, and the more love felt for this spot on earth. That love reflected on the sea wall along the Esplanade, which was decorated with hundreds of tiles, hand painted by people of all ages, all who agreed that this was paradise. For me, yes, it was.

Here was where Gayle and I learned how to surf on actual surf boards, standing for only a second, propelled by nothing but the wave and ourselves. Here was where Mike captured breathtaking photos of the flowers with the morning dew along the Soquel River path. Here was where I played in the sand with Rowan and watched her jump a wave for the first time, her squeal of excitement imprinted in my mind forever. Here was where my mom, Gayle, Amy, Rowan and I danced during the Twilight Concert along with dozens of others, not caring how silly we looked. Here was where I repeatedly dropped money at In the Raw, a clothing store owned by a very tall man named

Harleen, who we privately refer to as the "happy Indian guy," who looked like he could be from Pakistan, but was actually from India. He radiated positivity like no other and always gave me a huge hug like he remembered me year after year.

Here was where I never got tired of watching the surfers catch a wave. Here was where I enjoyed a morning walk along the river path through Capitola Village, stopped at a coffee shop to get my favorite chai, then continued along the Esplanade and up the long flight of stairs to the top of Depot Hill, and dreamed of owning one of the few houses along the edge of the cliff with amazing water views. Here was where we took a drive to Big Basin Redwoods State Park where we hiked among the giant redwoods.

The tallest trees on earth. Like walking the streets of Manhattan, but with skyscrapers formed from bark, branches, and leaves. Towers stretched up with strength, but along the path we hiked, some were horizontal and broken into pieces, revealing an unexpected brittleness. A few stood hollow. Known as *chimney trees*, these ones had been tested against several dozen fires, until finally the burning had reached their heartwood through cracks in the bark. Their caverns provided shelter for black bears and bats.

The biggest chimney tree appeared as we turned a corner. Rowan ran right in, Amy followed her. Gayle took her turn after they exited.

I stood back and remembered, not cardboard boxes, but the tree whose root I sat upon as a child, whose scarred trunk allowed squirrels and chipmunks to scurry in and out. The colorful autumn leaves I collected. The thick bark I traced with my fingers. The tree I loved. The one I missed. I wondered what it had looked like on the inside.

I wondered. I breathed. I remembered the sunny days. The still days. The days that didn't want to move. I stepped into the chimney tree. I turned around. I traced the smooth, charred bark with my fingers. I breathed again. I looked up at the blue sky, a tiny dot at the top of the tree . . . and felt peace.

All these incredible memories surfed through my mind as I inhaled the salt air on Manresa State Beach. I reached for another sand dollar, a tiny one, still amazed that we found so many. My hands were almost full. Another one appeared a few feet away. I couldn't believe how easy these were to find. Just as I was about to pick it up, Rowan ran toward me, her hand outstretched.

"Aunt Sooozie! Aunt Sooozie!"

"Find another one?" I asked.

She smiled and opened her hand, revealing a perfectly smooth, pale blue-green piece of sea glass.

Acknowledgments

AS A FIRST TIME WRITER, I had no idea what writing a book involved. I am tremendously grateful for everyone I encountered along my journey.

Thank you to the many people who heard I was writing this book and felt the need to share their PTSD story with me. I admire your bravery and appreciate how difficult it is to speak about your trauma. This book is for you. Never lose hope that your life can get better.

All the members of *Peace with PTSD*, it is an honor to be in your company and I deeply appreciate the positive energy you bring to our group.

Stephanie Gunning, from the beginning you embraced my pitch and gave me confidence when you told me my manuscript had a lot of value. You pushed me to dig deeper, praised me when I found clarity and gave me wonderful advice at every step. I am deeply grateful to have connected with you.

Gus Yoo, thank you for designing a beautiful cover, one that is leaps and bounds better than the one I had pictured in my mind for the last four years.

Dan Poblocki, Judy Thomas, James Lavin, Karen Korinda, Karen Graf, Chris Graf and Lori Lynn Meader for reading the first versions of my manuscript. You all gave constructive criticism and advice, but more importantly, you all ensured me that I was going in the right direction.

The outstanding writers and mentors who attended the Sentences 6 conference at The Caspersen School of Graduate Studies at Drew University. You all had more influence on me and my writing that you'll ever know.

Meteorologist Dave Curren for providing me information on the storm, including satellite images.

Julia Egan, you are an incredible example of an amazing friend. Thank you for all of your help during this process and for always having an open door should Mike and I ever need to evacuate to your house.

My family for supporting my need to share my story even though it involves one of the most painful moments in our family's history. You have always been there for me, and I know I am so blessed to have you as my family.

My mom, my biggest cheerleader in all that I have ever done, thank you for constantly pouring belief into me. Though you weren't able to read this final version, I am sure you are celebrating in your afterlife along with dad, and I know he is relieved to know that his accident has now been turned into a force for good.

Finally, my husband Mike. Thank you for listening when I needed to share, for understanding when I needed time to write and for finding a way to make me smile again when I was feeling down. I could not have asked for a better husband.

ABOUT THE AUTHOR

SUSANNAH PITMAN was born and raised in northern New Jersey. She received her Bachelor of Science degree from Syracuse University and her Master of Science degree from Tri-State College of Acupuncture. She maintains a private acupuncture practice in Boonton, New Jersey. Her articles on PTSD can be found in *HuffPost* and *PTSDJournal*. In her spare time, Susannah enjoys running half marathons, hiking, cooking and traveling with her husband to Mexico, California, and Vermont.

Made in the USA
Columbia, SC
20 October 2018